Asprey

Competitive RIDING

Consultant

Jane Kidd

David & Charles

A DAVID & CHARLES BOOK

First published in the UK in 2000

A catalogue record for this book is available from the British Library

ISBN 0 7153 1086 0

Designed, edited and produced by Eaglemoss Publications Ltd, based on the partwork *Horse Sense*

Front cover photograph: Kit Houghton

Printed in the Slovak Republic for David & Charles, Brunel House, Newton Abbot, Devon

10 9 8 7 6 5 4 3 2 1

CONTENTS

1: Schooling and Jumping

Training a young horse • Flatwork: on the bit • Home schooling programme • Gymnastic jumping training • Gymnastic jumping: angles • Fitness for gymkhanas and show jumping • Preparing for showing and dressage • Preparing for work • Warming up for jumping • Jumping a course • Problem solver: refusals • Flatwork: pace variations • Fitness plans for eventing and hunting

Pages 6–71

2: Mounted Games

The fun of mounted games • Mounted games know-how • Mounted games: training • Mounted games: neck reining

Pages 72–89

3: Dressage

Introduction to dressage • The aids • The paces • Lateral work • Canter exercises • Dressage tests • Dressage test: on the day • Dressage test: improvements

Pages 90–127

4: Eventing

The challenge of eventing • Speed and endurance • Cross country • Jumping combinations • Cross-country problems • Cross-country fences • Cross-country problems: 2 • Eventing: show jumping

Pages 128–169

5: Western Riding

First Western riding lesson • Tacking up • Western gaits • Neck reining, reining back

Pages 170–187

6: Endurance Riding

Introduction • Taking part • Endurance riding: training • Endurance riding: competing

Pages 188–205

Index
Pages 206–208

Picture Acknowledgements
Page 208

1: Schooling and Jumping

Training a young horse

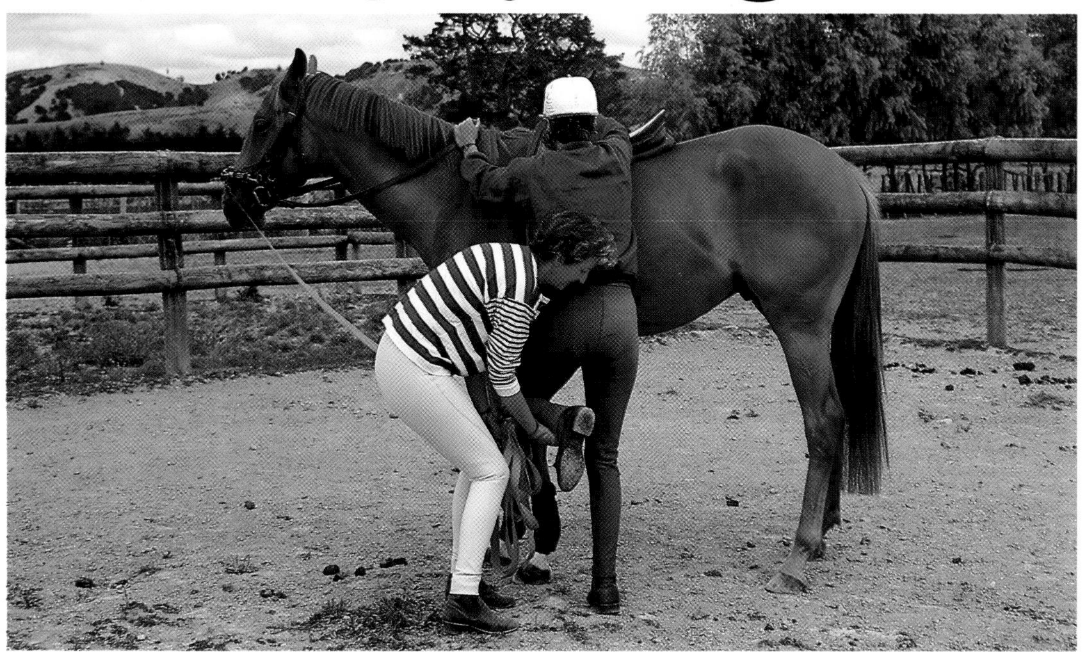

◄ **Teach the horse** to stand while you mount right from the beginning. Make it easy for him by either having a leg up or springing lightly and quietly into the saddle. Sit down gently and avoid having tight reins.

▼ **For the first trot,** it is usually better to rise than sit. This prevents stiffening in the back, and is less tiring.

A young horse's attitude to work is formed right at the very beginning. If he is broken in kindly and correctly, so that he looks forward to his training sessions, he has every chance of going on successfully. If this stage is done badly, leaving him frightened, insecure, angry or just confused, he'll never forget and will always be hard to train.

Before work starts

Before a young horse starts work, he has had plenty of freedom. Probably, he has not been asked to concentrate on anything for more than a few minutes at a time. Now he is expected to give full concentration for 20 minutes, with the time increasing as he grows fitter and more mature. Some horses find this very hard and need patient handling!

Another built-in difficulty is for the pony to accept orders from the region of his back. In the wild, anything on his back would have been a predator, to be shaken off as quickly as possible!

Hopefully, this early stage has been accomplished without a fright. Taken slowly, with plenty of reassurance from familiar people, he should now accept the weight and position of the rider.

The newly broken-in pony

It is not necessary to work a young horse every day. Very often, horses learn just as quickly in two or perhaps three sessions a week.

Try to finish each one when the pony has done something correctly, even if there doesn't seem to have been much progress. Reward is better than punishment and, in the end, speeds progress. Avoid doing too much. He is more likely to look forward to his next lesson if you stop while he wants to do more.

It's a good idea to begin each lesson with a little work on both reins on the lunge. This makes sure the pony is happy with his tack (particularly the girth), lets him loosen up, tunes him in to the trainer so he is ready to concentrate, and works off any freshness. Five minutes each way should be enough, but don't mount until he is ready.

Standing for too long is difficult for ➤

➤ **The rider** should keep her aids light when there is a trainer doing the lungeing.

WHAT BIT TO USE

▲ **During the early stages,** an ordinary jointed, eggbutt or loose-ring snaffle is usually used unless you have a reason to change.

▲ **'Breaking' snaffles** with keys encourage too much fussing and, in any case, it is better not to have to change the bit when the horse is ready to school on.

▲ **The French bridoon** is a less severe double-jointed snaffle than, say, the Dr Bristol.

▲ **A German, hollow mouth** is excellent as it is very mild, unless your horse has a particularly small mouth and finds this bit too large.

▲ **Rubber snaffles** tend to be chewed up and are only necessary for very soft-mouthed ponies.

young muscles so, if your girth was tightened before mounting and your stirrups adjusted, you can move away after just a few seconds. Some horses can be easily frightened if you shift around adjusting everything straight away: always move quietly, carefully and with plenty of reassurance. Make sure it is your idea to walk on and not his!

Teaching the aids

To teach the aids correctly requires two people, the rider and someone to lunge the horse. The person on the ground should already be used to lungeing him. The trainer gives the usual voice command to go forward while the rider, at the same time, gives a quiet aid by closing her legs. Gradually, with each repetition, the rider takes over. The leg aid is then *backed up* by the voice until the horse understands and no longer needs the voice command.

If the horse doesn't respond, it is because he does not understand. This is why the trainer on the ground is important. The same idea is used for teaching all the basic aids.

When you want to halt, remember that pulling the reins makes the horse pull at you, and teaches him to resist the hand. All that's needed is a gentle opening and closing of the fingers and a slight bracing of the back – and the trainer's voice until he understands.

At all times, keep your legs softly round the horse's sides, ready to ride forward. If you are prepared to take plenty of time over this stage, you'll be amazed how quickly your horse learns! Be careful not to do too much in one day, or he may suddenly lose concentration and do everything wrong.

Leave trotting until walk and halt aids are established. Then practise transitions from walk to trot and back on both reins before you attempt to move on to turning or think about coming off the lunge.

Learning to turn

Learning to turn may take a little longer than the first lessons in control. Again, a lot depends on patient, tactful and thoughtful riding. The horse should still be on the lunge, but the trainer should treat it more like a leading rein.

If you have space, and few disturbances, go for a walk away from the lunge circle. Applying the aids as for a trained horse, backed up by the trainer, make gentle turns in both directions.

It is vital to maintain a light contact on the outside rein, keep the hands level, and have no backward feel on the inside rein. The rider should turn herself, hips, body, shoulders and head, in the direction she wishes to follow and *push* the horse gently but firmly into the turn with her legs.

It's at this stage, when he's grasping the idea that legs, hands and body mean more than just 'stop' or 'go', that the horse begins to accept with real understanding the contact on his mouth from the rider. If he does become confused, the rider must stay relaxed but alert. He needs reassurance but not bullying! Soon he'll be ready to come off the lunge and start working independently.

◄ **Once the horse** fully understands the aids for walk, trot, halt and turn, he can begin work off the lunge. But don't rush these early stages.

▼ **Time to relax** is important if the pony is to benefit from his training. Young horses in particular find it hard to concentrate for any length of time, and enjoy the freedom of a field after working.

In his early training under saddle, a young horse should learn the basic aids to walk, halt and trot, and to make easy turns to the left and right. Provided the rider stays calm and sympathetic, this stage should not take too long. The next phase of his schooling demands a little more mutual concentration and trust.

First steps

Once your horse is used to a rider on his back and has learnt to obey the basic commands, you can move on to more demanding exercises. You must be sure he is ready to perform simple routines confidently and without fuss, and understands that his rider is in charge.

Strange new world

Youngsters are curious by nature and easily frightened. When your pony ventures into the wide open space of a field, or out on his first hack, he should be ready to listen to his rider. Even if he can see new and exciting things, or is asked to work where he used to play, he should remain attentive and obedient.

Young ponies enjoy the company of other horses and gain confidence from them when they meet strange objects. With this in mind, it is a good idea to get your youngster working in company before venturing outside the arena. Walk him quietly with another horse. If you don't have anyone else to ride with, a person on foot is the next best thing.

Walkabout

To start with, walk him round a large field or the yard where he's stabled, allowing him to look at new or strange objects without backing off or shying away. Once he has had a good look, let him go past without making a detour. Soon he will learn that if you, his teacher, are not afraid of unfamiliar objects he has nothing to fear.

Stop for a few moments occasionally so that he learns not to be in a hurry all the time. He has to understand that his rider is still in command and that he mustn't follow the lead horse blindly. Never get angry at this stage, but be firm and patient. When a young horse is tired or bored he may feel like arguing, so make sure the sessions are short.

As soon as you have reached the stage

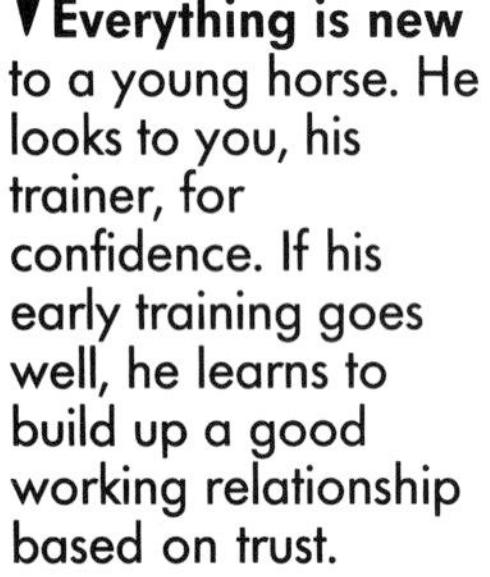

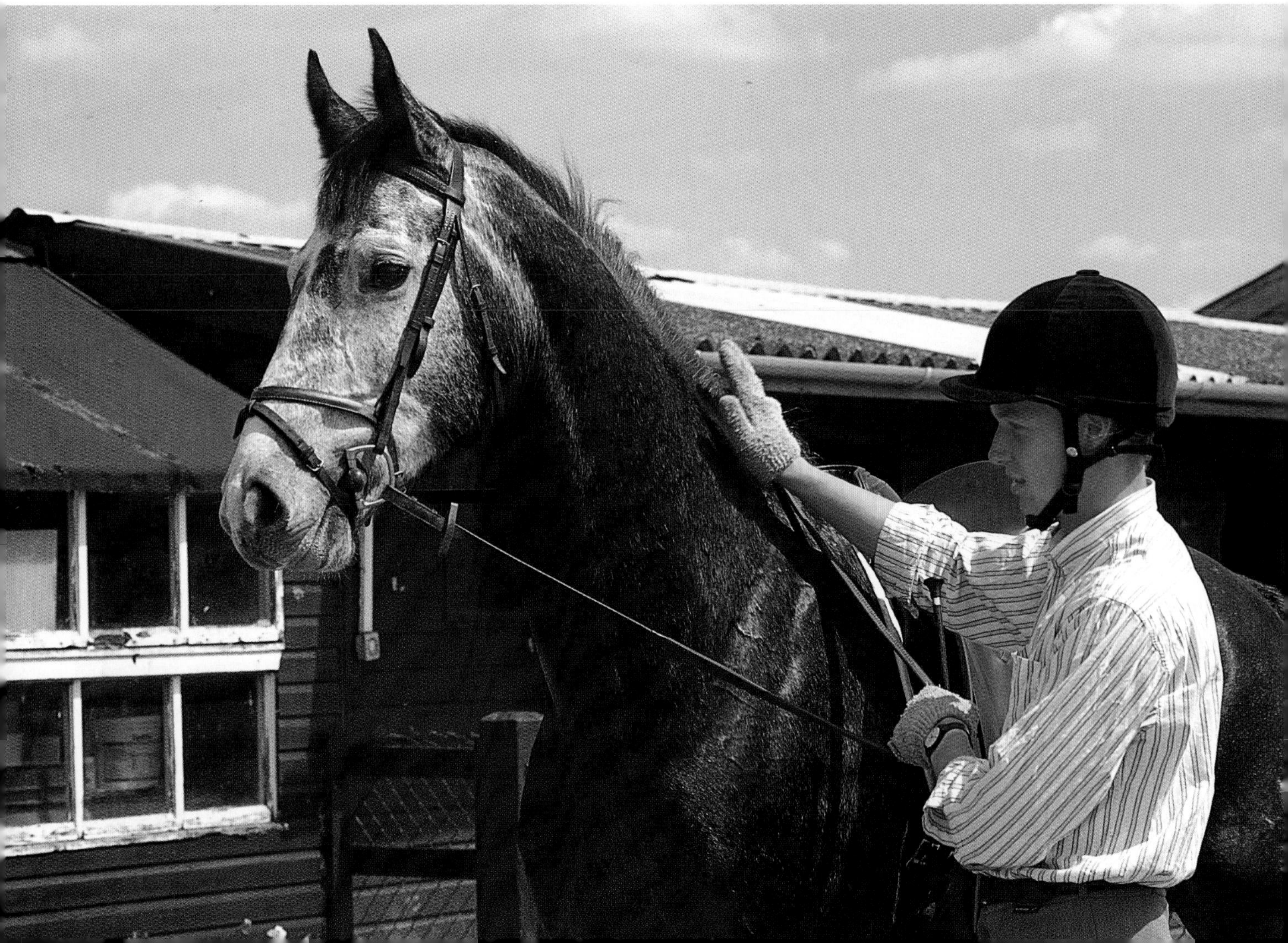

▼ **Everything is new** to a young horse. He looks to you, his trainer, for confidence. If his early training goes well, he learns to build up a good working relationship based on trust.

where you can walk him anywhere calmly, you are ready to start trotting. Then both of you can look forward to little expeditions. Stay alert – young horses can be unpredictable – and don't ride alone yet, in case there's an accident.

Lesson time

Schooling sessions are important, don't neglect them. It's a good idea to work in the arena for 10-15 minutes to settle him before going out. Later on, you can alternate hacking with schooling.

In the ring, introduce more circles and changes of direction in both walk and trot so that the horse develops the right muscles for strength and suppleness. In walk, decrease the size of your circles gradually from 20m to 10m in either direction. Try out simple manoeuvres, such as turning in a half circle to go in the opposite direction.

Practise the walk to halt to walk transitions and make sure he doesn't veer sideways. Use your imagination to make as many different patterns around the arena as possible, with plenty of changes of direction. Repetitive circling can bore a young horse and make him sour.

▲ **In the early stages** of training, it is a good idea to have someone with you, either on foot or on horseback, when you ride him out. Don't be lulled into a false sense of security and start riding out alone too early – if something goes wrong, you could both lose confidence in each other.

◄ **Introduce your young horse** to unfamiliar objects. Let him see how unafraid you are. He soon takes comfort from your calmness and learns that there is no reason to get spooked or agitated.

has never learned to gallop off with a rider, bolting is unlikely to be a problem, so don't anticipate trouble.

The first canter should be short, on the level or slightly uphill and should go away from home. He needs plenty of room at first, so leave cantering in the arena until he can go easily in the open. Whenever he hots up, return to a calm walk. If he is taught well and patiently at this stage, there is no need for your young horse to become over-excitable whenever his feet touch grass in the future – this is an irritating habit.

Quietly confident

As long as you remain calm at all times and see each lesson through to the right conclusion, progress will be very quick. Keep lessons short, simple and stimulating, and finish while the horse is still

◄**Most youngsters** find their lessons enjoyable. They become fidgety only when they are bored. As soon as your horse has done what you want without fuss, reward him for his effort then call it a day.

▼**The first venture** into the wide world is best made in a large field. Let your young pony look around as much as he wants. Keep him going at a steady walk until you are both sure you can handle a faster pace.

On the trot

Trotwork should be active but not fast. Maintain a steady rhythm at all times. When he can trot large circles easily, move on to figures of eight and loops and serpentines. His ability to hold both rhythm and impulsion will tell you how tight to make the turns. Generally, an 18-20m circle, a 15m half circle or a shallow loop of 3-5m down the long side of the arena is tight enough at this stage. Slow to a walk for a few strides if he loses balance or goes off course.

Using leg aids and slightly shifting your weight encourages him to turn – don't pull him round with the rein. Keep an even contact on his mouth to give him a chance to accept the bit.

Pick up speed

Cantering is best introduced on a hack, preferably following a friend. In active trot, you should feel a moment when the horse wants to canter. Sit down in the saddle, give the aid to canter and then let him do it himself without rushing. As he

enjoying himself and keen to do more.

It's a good idea to work out a rough weekly programme of schooling and hacking as long as you remain flexible and don't try to stick too rigidly to it. If your pony doesn't feel like doing something, don't force him. Some days he may be too tired to school, on others, windy weather or sheer high spirits may make him too excitable to work without a battle. If neither of you feels like a schooling session, go out for a ride that day instead.

Learning must be enjoyable for both of you. If you feel nervous about something, leave it until you have had chance to ask an instructor for help, otherwise your anxiety may well pass through to the horse. If you're feeling insecure, dismount and lead him. This is not a sign of failure: it may avoid an argument and helps the horse to feel confident with you. Teach through reward, not punishment, so your youngster is anxious to please and not frightened of disobeying you. He should regard training as fun.

▼ **Introduce the canter** when you're out in an open space. There is no reason for the young horse to become over-excited by fast work. He is too innocent to think about galloping off and dispensing with his rider!

Flatwork: on the bit

The expression 'on the bit' is one which everyone comes across sooner or later in their riding career. Many people think it means a supple poll and a vertical head carriage, but there is much more to it than that.

What it means

A horse is said to be on the bit when:

- His quarters are active and his hocks are engaged.
- He is in balance and rhythm, with a suppleness throughout his body, indicated by a swinging tail.
- He has a steady head carriage, with the poll at the highest point and the nose carried either vertically or just slightly in front of the vertical.
- He is working with a relaxed jaw.
- He accepts the bit with a light, elastic and even contact with the rider's hand.

Schooling

Because of conformation differences, some horses work more naturally and easily than others. Some may never be truly on the bit. Whatever his conformation, however, a horse can benefit greatly from basic schooling. He becomes obedient, free from resistances, and soon learns to work in total harmony with his rider. Even a stiff horse can become more supple with patient schooling on a regular basis.

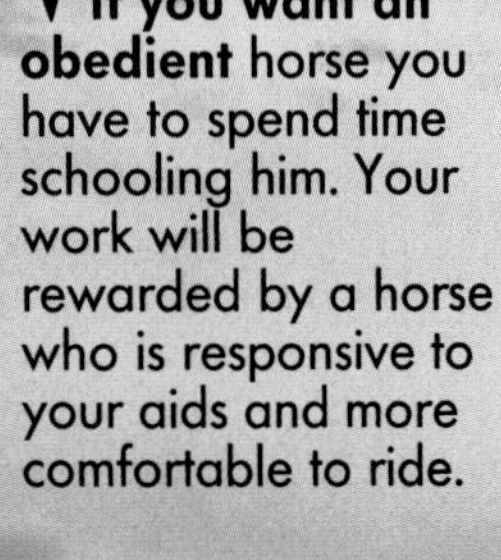

▼ **If you want an obedient** horse you have to spend time schooling him. Your work will be rewarded by a horse who is responsive to your aids and more comfortable to ride.

Impulsion

The horse's engine is in his quarters and before any work can begin, he must be using his back and quarters energetically, flexing his hocks and placing them well underneath him. He must go forward obediently to your leg, not run away from it.

The activity is created from behind and comes forward through a relaxed body, supple poll and relaxed jaw to your hands via the reins.

Straightness

Together with forward movement, the horse must be straight. His hindfeet should step into the marks left by his forefeet or in front of them (tracking up or over-tracking). You should also feel the same pressure on both reins.

On a circle, however, there should be a curve through the horse's body. Your inside leg should create the impulsion, while your outside rein and outside leg prevent his quarters swinging out.

Rhythm

A regular rhythm must be maintained if the horse is to achieve balance and a rounded outline. For an overall impression of smoothly flowing movement, the horse should be relaxed and swinging through his loins and quarters. He must not show any signs of resistance.

▲ **When a horse is on the bit,** his head is held either vertically or just in front of the vertical. The rider creates impulsion with her seat and legs and gives and takes with the reins. The horse relaxes his jaw and accepts the bit while working energetically from his quarters.

Thorough schooling

Problems arise when important school work has been hurried. Deal with them as and when they occur, since they won't just go away by themselves!

Work on straight lines, large circles and progressive transitions – all in rhythm and balance – helps to engage the horse's quarters.

If you try to collect your horse without enough impulsion, or if you ride with a weak seat and strong hands, you may cause the horse (especially a lazy one) to come behind the vertical. In this case, work on creating impulsion while allowing the horse to take a more positive forward feel through the reins. Don't confuse impulsion with speed, which throws the horse out of balance.

LEARN THE BASICS

If you want to school your horse well, you must know what to aim for. The basics of correct schooling are:

- Controlled free forward movement
- Straightness
- Rhythm and relaxation
- Balance
- Outline
- Acceptance of the bit

Above the bit

Your horse may come above the bit and hollow his back in resistance, especially if you ride with a very strong seat. You need to encourage him to stretch and round his back muscles and become supple equally on both sides. To do this, concentrate on 20m circle work, three loop serpentines and shallow loops, and use half halts in preparation for any change of direction or pace.

Practise keeping off his back as much as possible – rising trot and sitting forward to canter, gradually taking up a lighter seat.

Most importantly, do not allow the horse to run away from your leg. He must maintain his rhythm and balance.

If the horse is not straight and tends to

Common problems

▲ **If your horse is *above the bit*** he holds his head high and hollows his back. This is probably because you are using your seat too strongly. Lighten your seat and ride your horse forward.

▲ **If your horse bends his head and neck** past the vertical he is *overbent.* You need to push him up to the bit by using your legs and seat while keeping a light contact with the reins.

▲ **If your horse arches his neck** with his chin toward his chest he is *behind the bit.* He may be afraid. Ride him forward in a mild bit with a light contact.

be stiff, he may tilt his head to avoid stretching stiff muscles. Start work on his good side, encouraging him to accept the contact on the outside rein. Leg yielding is a good exercise to push the horse into your outside hand.

While working on turns and circles, remember to ask your horse for a bend from poll to tail. Don't allow him to bend just in the neck.

Warming up

Be careful to work equally on both reins and bear in mind that a horse is likely to be stiffer some days than others. Always remember to warm up before schooling and to cool down after work to ensure that your horse's muscles don't stiffen up overnight.

Avoid too much repetitive work. Introduce trotting poles on a circle to encourage the horse to stretch his neck forward and down. Do some gymnastic jumping twice a week to keep your horse interested in his schooling.

If your horse still resists, despite correct riding, make sure that your tack fits properly. Check your horse's mouth for sharp or wolf teeth and make sure that you are feeding him right.

You could ask your vet to refer you to a qualified chiropractor. He can check your horse's neck, back and pelvis for the slight misalignments that can prevent a horse working well.

Remember, being on the bit is not an end in itself. It is a stage that the correctly schooled horse reaches during his training. Once it has been achieved you can begin more advanced work.

▼ **Horses and ponies must be ridden *forward*** from the rider's leg. They must have impulsion and move energetically whether they are doing flatwork or jumping.

Dressage horses are good examples of horses who are ridden on the bit. They are usually well built with strong hindquarters. They must be well balanced and obedient to the rider's aids.

Home schooling programme

To enjoy your riding to the full, you want a pony that is well mannered, supple, forward going and obedient. Some schooling is necessary to achieve this aim and, even with few facilities, there is plenty you can do to improve your pony's all-round performance.

How to begin

When you're starting your schooling programme it's helpful to take advice from a properly qualified riding instructor. A professional can assess your riding and your pony's natural ability and level of training. It's a good idea to return for 'top-up' lessons every month or so, to help you as you progress to more advanced movements.

On the lunge

Lungeing is an excellent way of keeping your pony fit and supple when your time and space are limited. Be aware, however, that it is hard work for a pony and he must already be in fairly fit condition before you start this type of schooling. Also bear in mind the strain on the pony's legs if your lunge circle has become boggy or hard with frost.

◄ **Schooling your pony** improves his balance and makes him more comfortable to ride, whether you want to compete or simply hack in the country.

Keep your lungeing sessions short – not more than about 20 minutes – making sure that you work the *same amount of time* on both reins.

Aim to have the pony working actively from his quarters up into a contact with the side-reins if you are using these. Don't use side-reins to force the pony into an outline – they should never be so short that his face comes behind the vertical. Adjust them so that they are just long enough to encourage him to round his back and seek down for the contact. Keep the side-reins of equal length on each side.

Schooling hacks

All ponies are different and some need more work than others – you must know your own pony. However, don't forget that you can do useful work while out hacking. In the relaxed atmosphere outside the arena you may find the pony more receptive to your commands than when you are struggling in the school.

One essential to remember while trotting is to change your diagonal regularly – riding the same number of strides on each diagonal. Most ponies prefer you to sit on a particular diagonal as they tend to be more supple on one side. It may seem strange at first to use the opposite one, but you must if your pony is to become straight and balanced.

As you trot along the track, decide

▼ **Your local riding** school may have an all-weather arena that you can use. The surface is specially designed for horses so that you can ride even if the ground is frosty.

which rein you are on (depending on your diagonal) and think about riding your pony forward from your inside leg to your outside hand. Ride him straight, encouraging him to take the contact with the bit and your hand.

Along bridleways or across fields you could try some leg-yielding two or three steps out from the side, ride straight for two or three steps and then leg-yield back to the side again. Do this in walk as well as trot. As you progress, you can use the hedges or fences as the outside track and practise steps in shoulder-in, travers or renvers. This is probably easiest after coming around a corner which serves as your preparatory circle. (*Never* try to do dressage movements on roads.)

If you have to stop on your hacks to open and close gates, take the opportunity to practise a turn about the forehand. Make a change of direction by asking for a quarter or half pirouette to encourage the pony to engage his hocks fully – this helps to keep him supple.

Such schooling sessions can be good fun and much more interesting for you both than confining yourselves to the dressage arena.

These exercises help the pony to become more supple and obedient as well as straightening him and improving his performance. Remember to let him relax, however, and don't spend the entire hack asking him to work.

Transitions

As you walk and trot along, think about the quality of your transitions, remembering that they should all be ridden *forward*. When you canter, ask for a particular lead and don't let the pony simply strike off on his favourite.

A few good canter paces followed by trot and walk and then more upward transitions make a stiff pony supple.

If frequent changes of pace excite him, you may need to work him a little more beforehand, or give the pony a good canter to settle him. The same goes in the school; if your pony is not in the frame of mind for work or is bursting out of his skin you can wake him up or settle him down by cantering in the forward seat until he's beginning to blow a bit.

Knowing what your pony needs is important here, as is taking professional advice from someone who can see you both working together. All riders, at whatever level, need a pair of eyes on the ground.

Warming up

The ideal schooling ground is an all-weather arena of 20 × 40m (66 × 132ft), with dressage markers. Riding schools usually have these facilities, so see if your local school hires its arena for winter use when conditions can be difficult at home.

If you are aiming at competition work, schooling hacks won't be enough and

▼ **Lungeing Australian style:** Work on the lunge is an excellent way to make your horse supple. It encourages him to bend correctly and accept a light contact with the bit. Try to incorporate lots of transitions into your lungeing sessions as they are particularly good for making your pony responsive and keeping him balanced.

you need to do more formal work.

Always remember to warm up your pony thoroughly before starting concentrated work. He is just like an athlete or gymnast who has to limber up so that his muscles are working at maximum efficiency.

Take a gradual contact through a series of large turns and circles. Make sure that you ride through each corner as though it is part of a circle. Use the inside leg to make him take a contact on the outside rein. As he begins to settle, you can take up the contact and go through your work programme. Practising the movements from a preliminary or novice dressage test is fun and gives you a helpful structure to work around.

It's just as important to allow your pony to cool down after a schooling session. Let him take the rein and stretch down his head and neck while trotting and walking large circles. If he stretches readily then you know he's worked hard!

Be critical of yourself and learn to 'feel' when the pony is going well or badly. If something doesn't seem to be working, leave it for a while and return to a simple exercise which you and your pony do well – be flexible in your approach. The time to finish a session is when schooling is going well – you should never end on a bad note. Remember that *you* may be the reason for a bad day, not your pony!

▲ **When out on roads,** you must put traffic awareness first and concentrate on schooling only when you are on bridleways or in open country.

Changing diagonals frequently while you're out hacking helps to prevent your pony becoming stiff on one side.

◄ **Opening gates from** horseback provides the opportunity to practise school movements such as turn on the forehand and rein back. It's also much less trouble for the rider than dismounting!

Gymnastic jumping training

EQUINE GYMNASIUM

All successful athletes, whether they are runners, jumpers, throwers, swimmers or tennis players, do some form of training in the gymnasium. This training is intended to improve their suppleness, agility, balance, co-ordination, strength and technique. This type of 'gymnastic' training is also very helpful to riders and horses. The riding school is the horse's gymnasium.

Once you are capable of riding in walk, trot and canter on the flat and up and down hills, it is time to advance your skills further. Gymnastic training improves not only your jumping technique, but your general horsemanship as well.

Introductory work

The best introduction to this type of work is to ride over three trotting poles on a flat piece of ground. Make sure the distance is correct for your pony: 1.2m (4ft) is about right for an average 14.2-hand pony, but an experienced instructor adjusts the distance to suit each individual – his size, paces and so on.

If the pony has never trotted over poles before it is best to start with one and then, when he is confident, go on to three. Avoid two poles, as ponies often try to jump over both of them together. An odd number of poles prevents this happening.

Approach the first pole at right angles and ride through the series in rising trot, in a steady rhythm, maintaining a good position and an even rein contact. You don't need to alter your position at all, but you should feel the increased 'spring' in the pony's step as he negotiates the line of poles.

Folding from the hips

The next stage is to add a small jump about 2.7m (9ft) away (again, for a 14.2-hand pony – adjust the distance according to your pony's height) from the last pole. Ask the pony to trot quietly, but energetically, through the poles and over the jump.

Keep your position and rein contact

through the poles, then fold the top part of your body softly forward – from the hips and not the waist – over the jump. This ensures that you go forward with the pony and aren't left behind as he makes the effort to jump.

As an extra precaution you could fit the pony with a neck strap, and slip one or two fingers through this to help you keep your balance.

The important points to remember are:

- you must remain relaxed and supple and not tense up
- keep a steady but allowing rein contact
- the position of your legs should stay the same
- the shape of your upper body should not change – keep it straight when you make your fold forward from the hips, and don't exaggerate the movement.

A second element

Build up the exercise further by adding a second jump. It helps to have some idea of the length of your pony's canter stride so that you can space the two elements correctly. This is when a trainer's experienced eye is most helpful: you don't want to ride straight into a problem at this early stage.

The distance between the two elements could be anything from 4–7m (15–23ft). A keen pony with a tendency to jump big needs a lot more room than a pony who is inclined to be lazy or over-cautious.

Begin by using your usual build-up exercises. Poles on the ground, trotting poles to a low cross-pole – whatever

Behind every successful partnership lies a thorough training programme. Gymnastic exercises are the starting point in the development of the complete, confident, competition rider.

settles and encourages your pony is correct for him.

Without altering the arrangement of poles and fence, simply add the second element, which should be the same as the first, allowing one canter stride between the two parts. He may be surprised to see another jump but, if it is correctly placed, there is no reason why he shouldn't pop over with all the confidence in the world.

If your trainer has taken the pony through each new stage by loose schooling, then this is the best way to start the new lesson. Once you have seen that all is well, you should be able to ride him through the same combination with no problems. Most ponies find jumping combinations great fun once they have the hang of it. Remember, as always, to stop before he is tired.

Raising the height

It's always exciting when you can start to raise the height of the jumps. Now that you and your pony can cope with a small double, have a go at something larger. Again, take your trainer's advice on distance.

Raising the second part of a double is the best way to help the pony take off in the right place. The first element is now acting as a placer for the second. Keep the first element low, so that he does not run out of impulsion at the second.

You will have to increase the distance a little between the two as the second part is raised. This allows your pony room to take off slightly farther back which will help him meet the extra height. A few centimetres (inches) difference in any one session is enough.

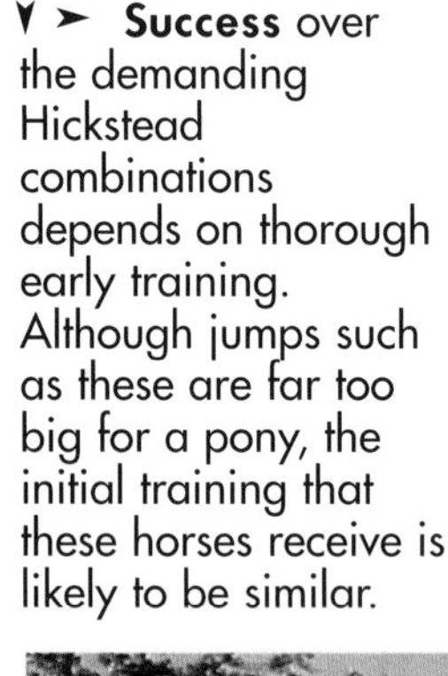

Success over the demanding Hickstead combinations depends on thorough early training. Although jumps such as these are far too big for a pony, the initial training that these horses receive is likely to be similar.

Cantering and circling

So far, the approach should have been in trot with perhaps one or two canter strides before take off if you are not using trotting poles.

Now try working for short periods in a steady canter. Canter a circle before approaching a low jump (placing a pole the stride before take off if it helps your pony). Canter in a straight line over your jump or combination and circle again afterwards, gradually returning to walk as you do so.

Walk on a long rein and relax. Cantering to a jump should not be exciting and lead to a loss of control. Riding calmly afterwards, to a plan and not aimlessly across a field until you run out of space, keeps your pony's concentration. It encourages him to think about your next set of commands. This is a great help when it comes to jumping a course.

Watching your trainer ride

Although you may feel relaxed riding your pony over jumps when he has learnt his lessons, watching your trainer teach him and other ponies shows you how to cope with difficulties in future.

➤ **Many ponies** jump beautifully at home, only to go to pieces at the first show. Now is the time to show the pony he can use his ability away from the security of home.

When out hacking, preferably with your trainer, look for fallen branches, logs or any other natural obstacle about the same height as the low fences your pony has already jumped.

Schooling with a friend or hiring facilities at a local yard also helps.

When the pony is ready to start jumping two or even three separate fences or combinations in succession, the trainer will make sure that the pony is always concentrating and ready to listen. To this end, it may be necessary to circle several times between jumps to regain balance, rhythm, obedience and/or impulsion.

The same technique can be used all through training so that the pony never develops the habit of a bad approach.

Each session must finish on a good note, even if it means going back a few stages occasionally to correct a fault. This way, the pony can look forward to his next lesson. Remember always to approach a fence riding forward,

First lessons in jumping combinations

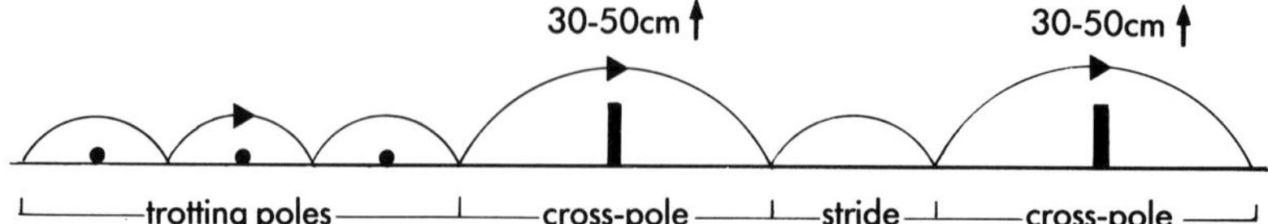

▲ **Introduce your pony to doubles** with three trotting poles, a cross-pole 30–50cm (12–20in), one non-jumping stride of canter and a second element to match the first. Approach in trot and finish in canter.

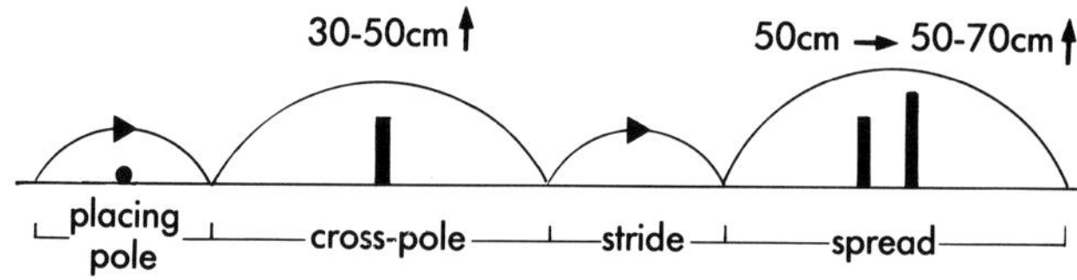

▲ **For the next stage,** use a placing pole the take-off stride before a cross-pole the same height as before. After one non-jumping stride in canter, increase the size of the second element to a width of 50cm (20in) and a height of 50–70cm (20–28in). Approach and follow through in canter.

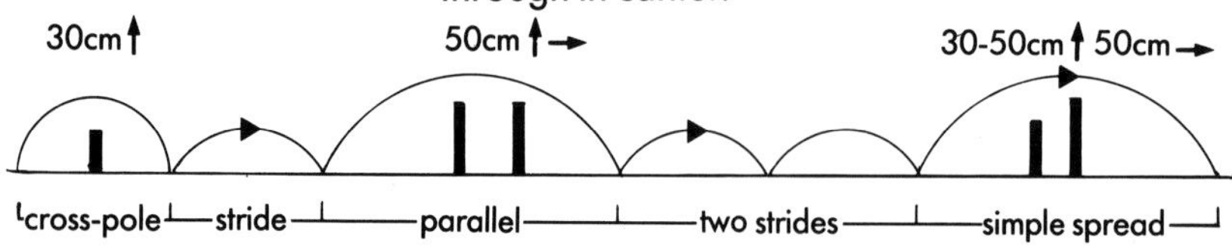

▲ **As the pony advances,** use a cross-pole as a placing fence, followed by one non-jumping stride of canter and a parallel 50cm high and wide. After two non-jumping strides of canter place an ascending spread, rising from 30cm to 50cm high and 50cm wide. This is a good follow-on exercise to use when the pony is jumping a simple combination well. The striding is worked out for him.

Using circles

Trot the first circle. When you arrive at the red arrow, you can see the centre of the poles and fence directly ahead. Decide whether to jump or whether to circle again depending on the readiness of the pony. Trot over the poles and cross-pole, with an optional canter afterwards. Re-establish trot

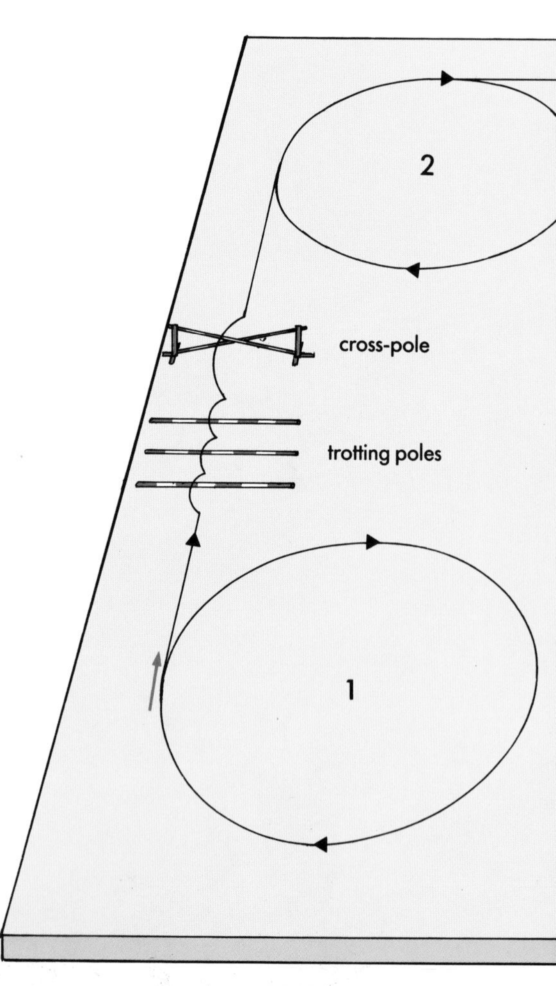

straight, calmly and with impulsion.

Seeing the stride

Adding a second fence is particularly helpful for teaching you to go with the pony, while maintaining a balanced position and steady rein contact. It also helps you to feel the rhythm of the stride on the approach to the jump, and to tell when the pony is going to take off. This is sometimes called seeing the stride, and is a very important part of jumping.

As your technique improves and the pony gains confidence, the exercise can be advanced by cutting down the distance between the jumps to 2.7–3.1m (9–10ft). Here the pony lands and takes off again straightaway and does

in the second circle, trot on to circle three which you should start in trot before taking up canter. Circle as many times as is necessary to obtain good balance and impulsion. When the pony is ready, continue over the pole and jump before re-establishing trot in the fourth circle. Reverse the whole exercise to work on the other rein.

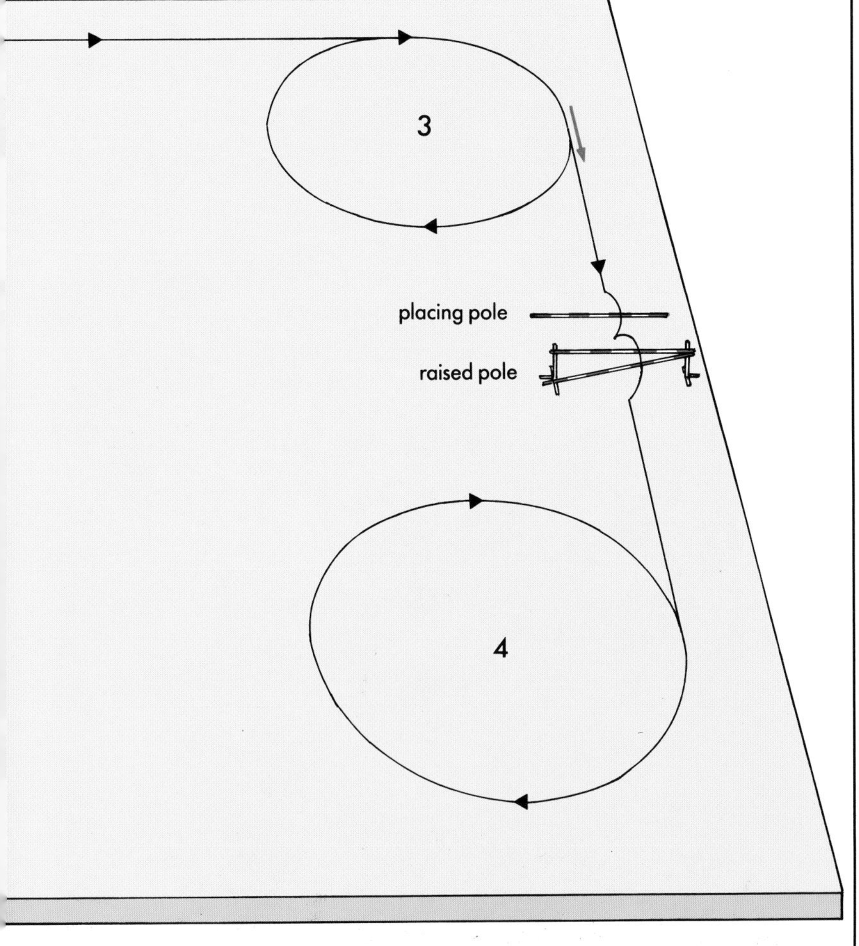

Loose jumping

Loose jumping is an excellent way of assessing a pony's natural ability. It also encourages the pony to think for himself and develop fluent style. Its advantage over lungeing is that there is no rein to be caught on a wing and no danger of pulling the pony's head round if he goes too fast. The only equipment you need is the usual protective boots, a headcollar and a lunge whip.

It takes plenty of skill and practice to be in the right place at the right time. Some ponies learn all too quickly to race on ahead and dodge the jumps or to duck back at the last minute. Having an assistant is advisable. Once they understand what's required, most ponies enjoy loose jumping and, with steady training and encouragement, happily clear quite large jumps in great style.

Loose jumping can only be done in an enclosed area with a good ground surface. The surrounding barrier should be high enough and solid enough so that the pony does not even think of jumping out. An indoor school is ideal. If the area is too large you'll need help to keep your pony travelling in the right direction or you will use all your energy racing up and down!

not take the canter stride. This is referred to as a *bounce* between the jumps, and calls for extra suppleness, balance and 'feel' from the rider.

A great variety of exercises can be made up along these lines. The next stage could be to use three trotting poles at 1.2m (4ft) distance, a gap of 2.7m (9ft) then a cross-pole at about 45cm (18in), a gap of 2.7m to make a bounce and another cross-pole at 45cm, followed by a gap of 5.5-6.1m (18-20ft) to give one canter stride and finally a small brush fence at about 60cm (2ft).

The object here is to give the rider training in maintaining a balanced position while going forward with his horse, keeping good rein and leg contact – in

1 Begin your gymnastic training using trotting poles. Keep a steady rhythm, and don't be tempted to change your position as the pony picks his feet up over the poles.

2 Add a small jump at the end of the line of poles. The only movement you make is to fold your upper body straight forward from the hips – not the waist or you hunch your back.

3 Add a second jump one canter stride from the first, then as you progress cut the distance between the jumps down to make a 'bounce' combination (no canter stride). Concentrate on maintaining your position and balance so that you stay *with* the pony instead of getting left behind, and beware of trying to 'lift' him over the second fence. This exercise helps you to develop a good *feel* for the pony's jump, as he lands and takes off again immediately.

▲ **Jumping a line of fences one canter stride apart:**
● The rider looks straight ahead throughout the exercise.
● A soft, sure but 'allowing' rein contact is maintained, together with the straight line from the elbow through the little finger, down the rein to the horse's mouth.
● The lower leg, from the knee downward, remains still and in the correct position.
● The shape of the upper part of the rider's body remains the same.
● The upper part of the rider's body is inclined softly forward from the hips, not from the waist which would round the back.

fact, keeping the horse 'between leg and hand'.

Jumping without reins

When you are skilled at riding these exercises, you can prove the independence of your seat by riding them without the reins. Tie a knot in the reins so they can't fall down around the pony's legs.

As you approach the trotting poles, drop the reins on the pony's neck, fold your arms lightly across your chest, and ride through the exercise in the normal way. This shows that you are not relying on the reins for balance. After the last fence quietly take up the reins again and ride forward.

The logical sequence to this is that the rider, *when experienced enough*, does the exercise without reins or stirrups to develop his balance and confidence. This must only be done under the supervision of a qualified instructor, but is a valuable part of the gymnastic training of a competition rider.

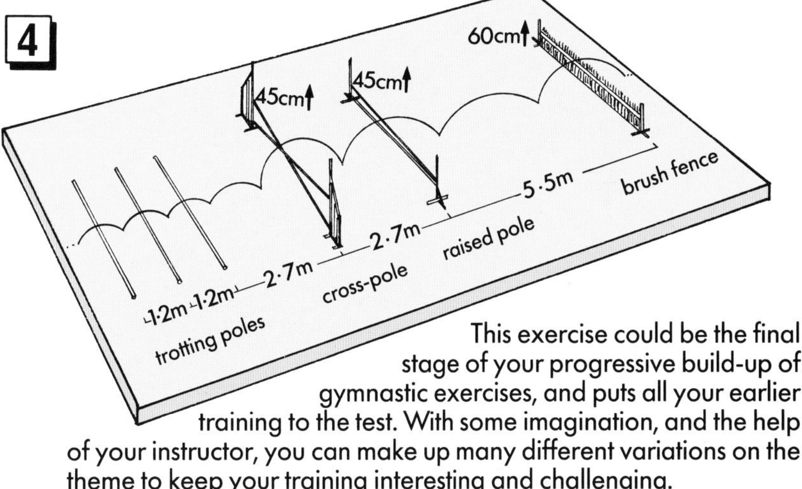

This exercise could be the final stage of your progressive build-up of gymnastic exercises, and puts all your earlier training to the test. With some imagination, and the help of your instructor, you can make up many different variations on the theme to keep your training interesting and challenging.

Gymnastic training: angles

▼ **You can help** your pony to turn simply by looking toward the next jump. If you look to the left when you want to turn left, the pony is more likely to land on the left leg and so be ready to turn.

Once you and your pony can quietly jump a series of small fences in a line you are ready to move on to the next stage of gymnastic jumping. This involves jumping fences at an angle – riding curves to the left and right and eventually making some turns. By jumping practice fences in this way you learn how to guide your pony through turns – essential when you take part in competitions.

Stage A – a line

Stage A can be set up in an indoor riding school, a manège or paddock. Remember to measure the distances properly when building the course. For this exercise keep the trotting poles 1.2m (4ft) apart. Leave a gap of about 2.7m (9ft) between the poles and the first jump. The distance between jumps 1-2 and 2-4 is 5.5-6.1m (18-20ft). These distances are based on a 14.2-hand pony. Ask an

instructor to help you adjust them to suit your pony.

Before you start jumping, warm up by doing some flatwork for 15 minutes or so. You can ride the first exercise in four progressive stages.

Start by approaching the trotting poles in an active working trot, rising. Trot through the poles, jump fence 1, take three strides in canter (passing between fences 2 and 3) and jump fence 4.

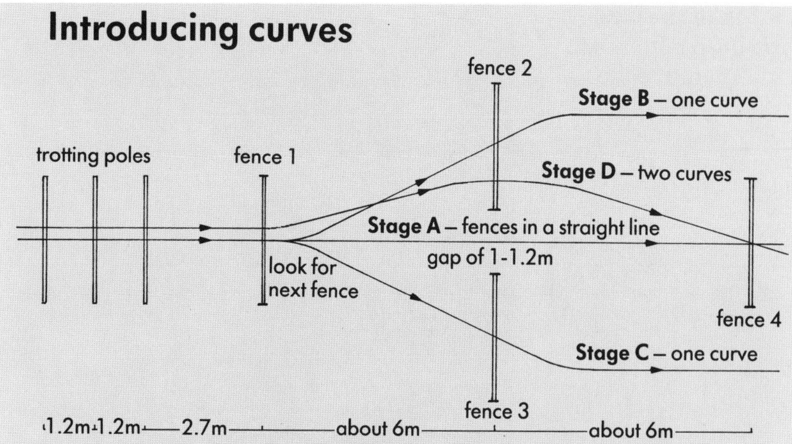

From a straight line of jumps (**Stage A**), you can gradually progress to one curve (**Stages B and C**) and then two curves (**Stage D**). Always look ahead for your next fence and try to keep the pony's pace even throughout the exercise.

Quietly bring your pony back to the working trot and when you are balanced and ready, bring him in to the exercise on the other rein. Always do the exercises equally on both reins.

Stages B and C – angles

Stage B includes a slight turn. Start on the left rein and trot through the poles. Look at the centre of the pole in fence 2 and jump fence 1. Feel the left rein and keep your right leg close to your pony's side. Take one stride in canter and jump fence 2. This means that you jump at a slight angle which is good training for when you have to jump a course fast, in a timed jump off for instance. When you have jumped fence 2 come quietly back to trot and, when you are ready, repeat the exercise.

Stage C is the same as Stage B except that you curve the other way. Start on the right rein, trot through the poles and jump fences 1 and 3. This time keep your *left* leg against the pony's side. This is probably enough for the first day's training in these exercises.

Stage D – two curves

In the next session, repeat the first three stages before you start the next jumping exercise.

Stage D involves two curves so keep looking ahead for your next jump. Make sure you keep your legs in contact with the pony's sides to prevent him running out.

Start on the left rein and trot through the poles, a little to the left of centre. Jump fence 1 looking at fence 2. Take

★ LOOK AND LEARN

You can learn useful skills from this work – it helps you to:

- Look and think ahead.
- Keep the pony between the leg and the hand when jumping a course.
- Jump a fence at an angle.
- Feel for the rhythm and the pony's stride.

► **Make the fences** you build different to add interest to the course. Keep them fairly small and concentrate on jumping correctly.

▲ **When you build** your course remember that you must be able to jump each fence in both directions. So make sure that there are no sharp edges sticking out of either side of the fence.

▼ **Your pony** may find it odd to jump at an angle at first. Both you and the pony need to be balanced and alert.

one stride in canter and jump fence 2 while looking at fence 4. Then feel with the right rein and close both legs against the pony's sides. Take one stride in canter and jump fence 4.

Balance and control

If, after jumping fence 2 you find that you cannot jump fence 4 without a struggle, don't attempt it. Instead ride out the exercise as if you were practising Stage B. Recover your balance and control before trying again. It is very important to carry out these exercises in a quiet, balanced way, but with plenty of impulsion.

The final part of stage D is to repeat the exercise on the right rein, jumping the fences in the order 1-3-4.

Nearly all horses and ponies are stiffer one way than the other, so it is better to start work on the rein that the pony finds easier. When he is making progress on that rein change to his more difficult rein.

How to jump a course

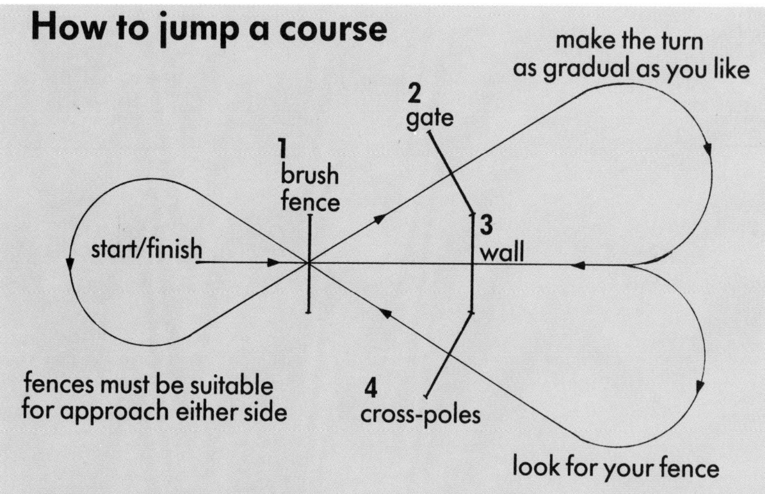

▲ Starting on the right rein, jump fences 1 and 3 as a double. Jump each fence in the centre and take one canter stride between them. As you jump fence 3 feel with your right rein and, when you land, start making a turn to the right looking at fence 4. Make the turns very gradual when you begin the exercise. It's better to jump the fences correctly than to do the course fast.

Approach fence 4 straight and jump it in the middle. Keep your pony straight and jump fence 1 at an angle. Jumping at an angle may seem strange at first. Keep the fences quite small so your pony doesn't take fright!

When you land, feel with your left rein and make a gradual turn to the left. As you turn, look at fence 1 and approach it at an angle. Keep your pony straight and jump fence 2 in the centre. As you land, feel with your right rein and make a right turn. Look at fence 3 and, approaching it straight, jump fences 3 and 1. Then repeat the exercise on the other rein.

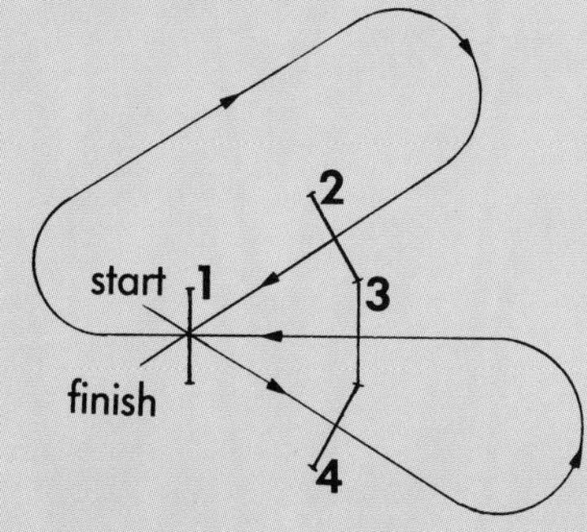

◄ You can jump this course in other ways. Just jump fence 1 at an angle; approach all the others straight. Start on the left rein and jump fence 1 at an angle and fence 4 straight. Then turn to the left and jump fences 3 and 1. Complete the exercise by turning right and jumping fences 2 and 1.

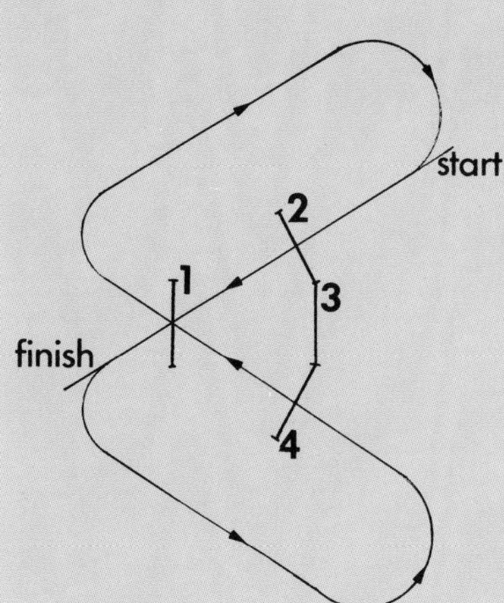

◄ Alternatively, you can try it this way: start on the left rein, and jump fences 2 and 1. When you land turn to the left and jump fences 4 and 1. Turn to the right and repeat the exercise on the right rein. This time you jump fences 2 and 1.

Jumping a course

The next exercise helps you to ride doubles well, and also teaches you to look ahead for your next jump. Lay the jumps out with 5.5-6.1m (18-20ft) for a 14.2-hand pony between the centres of 1 and 3; 1 and 2; and 1 and 4. Once again ask your instructor to help adjust these distances to suit your pony.

Make the fences look different. Number 1 could be a brush fence, 2 a gate, 3 a wall and 4 a cross-poles. Make sure that all the fences are 'jumpable' in both directions.

Ride the course slowly and carefully, concentrating on doing it well. You can take it in trot or canter but try to keep the pony between your leg and your hand throughout the exercise.

Use half halts to keep the pony well balanced, and make sure that he is bent in the direction in which he is going.

You can build variations of these courses with your instructor to help you and your pony jump in a fluent way.

Fitness for gymkhanas . . .

▲ **The gymkhana pony** needs to be agile and nimble, and to develop nerves of steel! Like his jumping counterpart, he needs to have strong legs and to be fit enough for sudden bursts of speed and energy.

Once you've decided that you want to do more than hacking or flatwork, your pony needs extra training. For either jumping or gymkhana games, you need to think about how your pony is going to be used and tailor your fitness programme to suit.

The two disciplines

Gymkhanas and jumping require boldness and agility. The tendons and ligaments

! WARNING SIGNS

Keep regular checks for heat and swelling on any part of the limbs. This may be the first sign that you have done too much. Look out also for sore backs and girth galls, loss of condition and loss of appetite. These are all signs that your pony cannot cope with the work.

. . . and show jumping

of all four legs need to be strong. The jumping pony lands hard on one of his forelegs after each jump; the gymkhana pony needs to stop in a very short distance. The jumping pony uses his hind limbs as he pushes up and over a fence; the gymkhana pony uses his in sharp turns and quick getaways.

Tendons and ligaments can only be as strong as the muscles which work them, so both types of pony need to be well muscled and powerful, with the muscles ready for short bursts of hard work. This is quite different from the long-distance pony, where the demands are for staying power rather than quick strength.

The type of pony

Many ponies compete in jumping and gymkhana classes with equal success, while others excel in either one or the other. A jumping pony needs to be

▼ **A pony** used for competitive jumping needs to be careful and bold. To coax the best performance from his naturally athletic build, he has to be schooled and exercised to a peak of fitness for about six weeks before a show.

calmer in his outlook and to be a real athlete. Courage is important. If he makes a mistake and hurts himself, he must be brave to carry on. The same applies if he meets a strange-looking jump or isn't sure that he can clear an obstacle.

The gymkhana pony does not need to face the same demands. He should be quick witted and intelligent, very agile and not put off by flapping objects, bright colours and loud bangs! He does not need the same high degree of courage. A gymkhana pony should be small; the best are generally well under 13 hands. A jumping pony can be up to 14.2 hands and is classified according to his height.

Fit for gymkhanas

Once your pony is fit for day-to-day riding, spend 10-15 minutes three or four times a week toning up his tendons, ligaments and muscles. He needs to learn how to stop and start over short distances without growing over-excited.

In stopping quickly, he braces his forelegs and also sits back on his haunches. It is a technique which needs to be learned and he will improve as he

◄ **The pony's fitness programme** must be backed up by a routine of caring stable management. Regular feeding, grooming and general checks are essential for stabled and outdoor ponies.

Training exercises

▲ **Bending** is good practice for gymkhana ponies as almost every game requires tight turns. Make the exercise more tricky by bringing the cones closer together and by going faster.

▲ **Provided that he is small enough**, a pony can be trained to perform at both jumping and mounted games. The cones also double up, as bending posts and jump fillers.

becomes stronger. Avoid pulling him hard in the mouth, as this will only upset and frighten him. A quick get-away also improves with practice but, again, take care not to do too much.

A good basic exercise to improve agility is bending. Set out a line of cones about 6m (20ft) apart. Go to the left of the first, right of the second and so on, gradually increasing your speed. Make your line as straight as possible, using your weight to move the pony just enough to clear the cones. As you both improve, you can bring the cones closer together.

Turning tightly at speed round a single cone is a knack used in almost every race. It is very demanding in strength and balance, so the pony needs building up gradually. The better your balance is, the better your pony's is.

Spend as much time as you can spare on strange sights and sounds. This is not going to tax your pony's body but may tax his mind! Never be angry with him if he tries to run away from bursting balloons or flappy washing lines. If you are patient and firm he will take confidence from you and learn quickly. If he is going to be any good, he must learn to enjoy himself so that the two of you can work together.

When you've spent two or three weeks on general technique and muscle toning, try to meet up with a group of friends for a weekly practice. *You* need training just as much as the pony, so that you can jump on and off at speed, ride one-handed and have a good eye for aiming things in buckets or drain pipes! Learn to carry objects from the saddle, run across stepping stones and jump along in a sack – while leading your pony!

Fit for jumping

From basic fitness, the jumping pony needs gradual building up in the same way as a gymkhana pony. If he hasn't jumped at all for a whole season, then start again with trotting poles and low fences.

Allow 4-6 weeks before his first competition if he can already cope with 1-1½ hours of light work. Two or three sessions a week is plenty. Gradually increase the height and difficulty of your fences and jump one or two as high as those on the competition day. This gives you confidence when you are away from home and may have 'ring nerves'.

If your pony is already experienced and capable of jumping against the clock, then build up his ability to turn quickly – in stages as for the gymkhana pony. If you take it too quickly, you run the risk of laming him at the beginning of the season.

Once you start to make short approaches and turns on landing, you find out just how much your pony has to offer and whether or not he is brave, agile and strong.

SHOEWEAR
Shoes wear down more quickly with hard work. Walking on the roads and some trotting tones up the legs and feet but also makes for more frequent shoeing. Watch out, too, for uneven wear. If this happens, talk to your farrier. You may have to change your work for a while.

▲ **Bales of straw** make a versatile jump that can be approached from either side, and lowered, raised or widened as required. Don't jump more than twice each way without a rest.

Preparing for . . .

A calm, obedient, forward-going pony in peak condition is a winning formula in any show-ring or dressage arena. It's a pleasure to watch, certain to catch the judge's eye and just reward for all the hard work you've put in. While showing and dressage don't require super-fitness, such a picture of harmony takes time to achieve at any level.

The type of pony

Generosity and good manners from any pony are worth their weight in gold. To be a true show pony, he must also have excellent conformation, balance, movement, quality and presence. No pony is perfect, however, and it's up to you to 'sell' your pony to the judge. Those first few minutes in the ring are critical if you are to be called in at the top of the line.

Straightness and unrestricted natural paces are musts for a dressage pony. Dressage also benefits other equestrian activities because it is a tough discipline requiring obedience, balance and acceptance of forward and restraining aids. The schooling you have to do improves the pony's performance in jumping, hunting and eventing as well.

Fit not fat

During the winter months, your pony is probably in fairly soft condition – well fed and rounded with little work – whether stabled or out at grass. In early spring you should start working on fitness for the summer.

You want the pony looking his best at the start of the showing season, without the tail-end of his winter coat. Start rugging him up at night to encourage him to lose his coat a little earlier than is natural, and to make grooming and strapping easier. If you have a stable, now is the time to start bringing him in. Make no sudden changes to the pony's diet or routine.

As your riding time becomes longer, increase the concentrates. The pony also

▼ **To gain good marks** in a dressage test, the pony needs to have rhythmic paces. He also needs to be reasonably fit, well schooled and obedient. If you are taking a Pony Club dressage test in summer, start preparing for it in early spring to give yourself a good chance of success.

. . . showing and dressage

◄ Teaching a pony to stand out is essential for the show ring. It takes practice to make him do it correctly. Remember to ask him to step *forward* into position – never push him back.

SHOWING CLASSES
Study the show schedules carefully and pick only those classes suitable for you and your pony's capabilities. Riding club pony and working hunter pony classes are best for those with less than perfect conformation. In-hand classes are ideal for youngsters as they give you both valuable experience.

needs hay until grazing value reaches its peak in early summer. Don't, on the other hand, let him gorge on lush spring grass. Apart from the risk of laminitis, fat is certainly not fit.

Never overfeed on concentrates. You want to be able to ride your pony. A fizzy bomb impresses no one – least of all the judges at the show.

Ready for shows

Unlike show-jumping or gymkhana ponies, the show pony has to stand still for long periods of time. He also needs to remain calm, happy and alert in the face of a barrage of sights and sounds.

Practise standing him out in the field. To do it correctly takes patience from both of you. If there's plenty going on around you, so much the better. No showground is empty!

Never push him back to make him stand out – the pony should take a step forward. Be careful that he is showing all four legs: hindlegs and forelegs should not be together. The foreleg on the judge's side should be slightly in advance of the other, and the nearest hindleg slightly behind the opposite one.

The pony needs to remain attentive. Crumple an empty sweet wrapper in your pocket or offer a few blades of grass in your hand. Both work wonders.

You will also need to walk the pony away and trot him back so the judge can assess correct movement. Practise keeping in a straight line. You should stay level with your pony's shoulder when trotting up and give him some rein so he can carry his head correctly, without any restrictions from you.

This needs practice. You don't want to be left miles behind, with the pony running over the judges on the way back! Neither should you drag your reluctant pony along. Quietly clicking with your

▼ Practise trotting up the pony in a straight line for the judge. You should be level with the pony's shoulder – not dragging him along or trying to restrain him.

tongue or a sharp tap with your show cane (out of hearing of the judge when you're in the ring) helps to drum up enthusiasm.

In ridden classes you also have to give a show. Plan in advance what you are going to do and take advantage of your pony's good points. Keep it short and always move off on your best rein. Above all, you need to look as if you are enjoying yourself during the show.

Schooling sessions

It's best to work a little and often. One 30-minute session a day, followed by half an hour's hack, is plenty to begin with. Long work periods, going round in aimless, repetitive circles, leave both you and the pony tired and bemused.

Before you start schooling, loosen up. Walk round on a long rein, and do some rising trot, frequently changing direction and diagonals. Do some canter work with you in the forward position to help the pony to stretch and supple up his back and hindquarters.

Then begin to work. Be clear in your own mind what you want to achieve during any schooling session. It might be

▲ **Loosen up** before schooling with some rising trot. Then work with a clear aim, such as making smoother transitions or improving the pony's bend on corners.

▼ **Allowing time** to relax with friends on a hack stops you and the pony becoming stale. You can still try to keep your pony alert and on the aids, between leg and hand.

➤ **Grazing in-hand** is appreciated by a stabled pony who has no other fresh food. If you can, let him loose in a paddock for part of each day, so he has some freedom.

smooth walk/trot/canter transitions, or well-shaped circles with the pony in a correct bend. Keeping your pony on the aids between leg and hand is a very good discipline for you both and helps with *accuracy* and *straightness*. Dressage judges are very keen on both.

Stop when you feel you've achieved your aim. Give the pony a long rein, pat him and let him stretch down. He deserves it. Good work should always be rewarded.

Vary your routine during each session and don't keep practising tests – your pony will start to anticipate movements and become stale. Alternate your flat-work with hacking out and work over trotting poles – anything that holds your pony's interest. Boredom itself can start posing all sorts of problems such as napping, inattentiveness and lack of impulsion.

When you've finished schooling don't just jump off. Walking off your pony is as important as the loosening up period. It gives your pony time to cool off and relax and leaves him in the right frame of mind to work for you again.

MORE ON FEEDING

As you increase the pony's work, so you must increase the proportion of concentrates in his feed. Remember though that the pony's weight has more bearing than height on how much to feed.

Preparing for work

▼**To prepare yourself** and your horse for a competition, warm up away from the hustle and bustle of the collecting and show rings. Walk on a longish rein to a quiet spot, where you can put the horse through his paces gently and calmly. Warming up can be done on your own or with a friend.

Warming up, sometimes called riding in, means preparing your pony for hard work by giving him gentle exercise first. This helps you to get the pony going smoothly and attentive to the aids. At a show, warming up encourages horses to ignore the bustle around them.

Well-oiled routine

All fitness-conscious humans know that it harms the body to go straight into strenuous activity. In an aerobics class, for example, everyone warms up slowly before the demanding routines start. This gentle preliminary exercise slightly increases the temperature of the muscles, helping them to function better during exercise. The idea is the same with a pony.

Warming up loosens up his muscles and tendons, which may be a little stiff and uncomfortable to begin with. Demanding active paces from the start could result in damage to the cold muscles. A pulled muscle or sprained tendon is a painful injury that can put a pony out of action for several months.

When a rider continually makes her horse get straight down to work without

riding him in, he learns to associate exercise with discomfort and becomes sour and evasive.

Riding in also helps you to detect any problems in your pony's demeanour, such as slight lameness or lack of spark, before you make extra demands on him.

Work that body

You can benefit from warming up, too. It is important to get your own muscles and tendons ready for riding and tuned to the task ahead. Warming up helps you to sink into the saddle close to your pony, and loosens up the riding muscles in your back and legs, which are different from the walking muscles you may have been using before you mounted.

▲**Canter on both reins** when warming up, but try not to do too much repetitive circle work. As he gets used to going forward at the canter, ask him to keep a soft, elastic rein contact and bring his hocks underneath him.

Fuel injection

A pony's body receives its fuel to work on from the nutrients in his food. These are carried in his bloodstream. When his food is digested, it passes from the stomach into the digestive system, where it is broken down into the various nutrients. They enter the bloodstream by tiny blood vessels called capillaries in the walls of the intestines.

Once in the bloodstream, the nutrients are carried to all the different parts of the body. They are converted into energy with the help of oxygen present in red blood cells.

The harder a pony works, the more energy he uses. To supply this energy, his body needs more nutrients and oxygen, and so more red blood cells. These are stored in the spleen. Cells are released when the spleen senses that the heart is beating faster and that the body is using up more fuel.

Releasing more blood cells takes time. Warming up provides that time by warning the spleen that activity is starting and that it has to get to work.

How to warm up

After you have mounted and gathered your reins, ask your pony to walk round on a long, even loose, rein. If the pony has been standing in a stable or trailer you should do this for a full five minutes – less if he has already been led around.

Next ask for a gentle trot on a longish rein, gradually taking up a little more contact and asking the pony to accept the bit. Try to get his hindlegs underneath him to stop him chugging around on the

KEEP YOUR COOL

If you are warming up before a competition or an important lesson, try not to let your anxiety transmit itself to your pony. If both of you are feeling jumpy you'll never be prepared for the task ahead. Try to tell yourself that warming up is the same as going out on a relaxing hack, and try not to dwell on the task ahead.

▲**An inquisitive pony** is distracted by the strange sights and sounds of the showground. If he is upset by all the action, warming up gradually encourages him to remember his training and forget his surroundings.

forehand. Keep to a rising trot at first and change the diagonal with every change of direction.

Stepping out smartly

Keep your pony interested. A bored pony refuses to co-operate or concentrate. Do figures of eight and use your imagination to vary the work. Depending on the progress he has made, ask your pony to do smaller circles, leg-yielding, loops and serpentines. Talk to your pony all the time, praise him for each good movement and calm him if he is over-fresh at the beginning.

If you are riding in a manège or school, make it a rule never to go round in endless, boring circles. Go across the middle of the school, down the centre line – anything to prevent repetition.

As he becomes more supple, gradually

➤**Jumping** excites a lively pony and requires high energy levels. Don't point your pony at any fences until you have warmed him up thoroughly to prepare him for the exertion.

ask for your pony's best outline. After about 15 minutes, finish off with some movements in canter on both reins. If you are jumping, try to avoid taking the practice fence any more than three times in each direction. Then call it a day, he should now be fit and ready for the serious work.

Light relief

Cooling down is as important as warming up. During work, the pony's fuel is burned up, a process which produces waste products in the muscles in much the same way as a car's engine burning petrol gives off exhaust fumes. The pony's blood needs time to absorb the waste products from the muscles and carry them away to be passed out in sweat, urine and droppings.

To allow your pony's body to dispose of waste products more quickly, bring him down gradually from fast, hard work. Never put your hot pony to bed straight after strenuous work or he'll feel stiff and uncomfortable in the morning. Instead, trot gently about for up to 10 minutes to keep the blood flowing and ridding itself of waste products. This gentle cooling down from fast work gives time for the blood to restore fresh energy supplies to the body, replacing those just used up.

Next, bring the pony to a walk for another 10 minutes, preferably in-hand. This relaxes him gradually. Give him small sips of water if possible. Loosen his girth and, if it is chilly, throw a rug over him. Let him have a short graze till he is completely relaxed, cool, dry and ready to be put away. Don't forget to check his feet and remove any sweat stains before you leave him for the night.

▼A gruelling cross-country course leaves a pony and his rider hot and over-excited. The cooling-down process is most important. After trotting gently to remove waste products from his system, the tired pony is walked in-hand to calm him.

Warming up for jumping

Like an athlete, a horse needs to be warmed up before he can produce a good performance. Jumping is more demanding than exercising on the flat so that, even during a training session at home, you must allow time for preparation.

At rest

When your pony is standing at rest, his whole body is 'slowed down'. He cannot suddenly be asked to jump a course of fences as soon as you get on him – he needs time to 'tune in'.

As the pony warms up, movement gradually becomes easier. His joints, stiff from standing still, become lubricated by a special fluid – like oil in a car engine – called *synovia* (joint oil). His heart pumps harder to keep his muscles supplied with oxygen so that they can work efficiently.

Hot or cold

The weather affects how long you spend warming up. Cold, damp days are the worst so give the pony more time. Cold air causes the small blood vessels near the skin surface to close down, reducing the blood supply to the muscles. Exercise boosts the circulation again and the muscles can work easily.

If your pony is clipped out then it may be necessary to keep one rug over his back for the first 10 to 15 minutes of working in.

On a cold day, gentle trotting is best to warm your pony up quickly. If it is hot, it is better to loosen him up in walk. Bear in mind that both you and your pony tire more easily in hot weather.

Loosening up

Start with work that your pony finds easy and relaxing. You want him to be calm and to concentrate on what he is doing. To begin with, keep your reins long (but not loose) so that his outline is long and low.

Gradually move from walk to trot to canter as he settles in each pace. Ride large circles with frequent changes of rein to let him settle in a steady rhythm, and to loosen up in his neck, back and limbs. As he begins to work more fluently, increase the difficulty of the turns and circles. After about 10 or 15 minutes of these exercises, return to walk and let him stretch his neck with loose reins for a few minutes.

Now take up the rein contact and ride him forward into a more collected outline. To jump well, your pony should have his hocks well under his body and work with plenty of impulsion.

Transitions from walk to canter and from canter to walk help to collect him. Reining back (walking backward) quietly for a few steps before riding forward again flexes the joints in his hindlegs and rounds his back. Both these exercises are good tests of obedience and concentration as well.

◄ **Before every jumping session,** allow time for flatwork exercises to warm your horse up. Only then can he perform his best for you.

▼ **Reining back** for a few steps places your pony's hocks further underneath his body, which helps to round his body outline in preparation for good jumping.

▲ **Gradually progress** from walk through to canter as your pony loosens up. Practise your forward jumping seat as you go.

▲ **Hacking out:** Try to include hacking in your regular work. Go out before or after jumping, either to warm up the pony or cool him off afterwards. Returning your pony to the stable calm and dry after work is just as important as warming up correctly.

If you hack out before jumping, allow at least five minutes' schooling before you start to jump. This is a good time to use the direct transitions from walk to canter with no trotting.

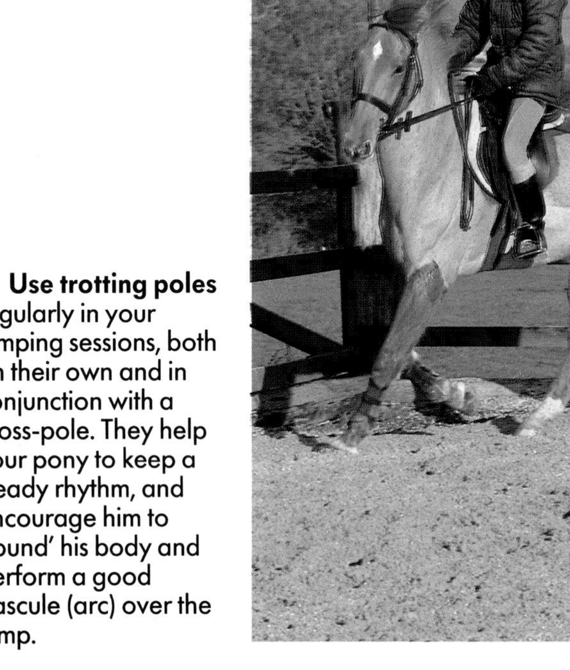

➤ **Circles and turns** are good suppling exercises for removing the stiffness in your pony's back, neck and legs.

▼ **Use trotting poles** regularly in your jumping sessions, both on their own and in conjunction with a cross-pole. They help your pony to keep a steady rhythm, and encourage him to 'round' his body and perform a good bascule (arc) over the jump.

Working over poles

Try to vary your warming-up routine as much as possible without taking any short cuts. About once a week, go back to basics and use trotting poles – as many as six in a line. Approach from either a straight line or a circle, keeping your pony slow but powerful.

Work over the poles until your pony is consistent in his rhythm. Then move the last two poles together to form a cross-pole, low at first so that he just trots over it. The cross-pole can gradually be raised to form a jump.

Approaching the jump in trot keeps the pony steady but really makes him work and develop a good 'bascule' (the rounded arc the horse makes when he jumps correctly).

On another day this routine can be varied so that you have one pole in front of the fence to place your pony correctly. Keep the jump small and later on place a bigger fence one canter stride after the first. Ride calmly into a circle after landing, settle your pony in trot and then repeat the exercise a few times – but not so often he gets bored.

At a show

By the time you get your pony to his first show, you should know how long it takes to warm him up and which exercises suit him best. Allow one hour more than you would at home so he has time to adjust to his surroundings.

You don't need to ride him for the whole hour (which would wear him out!) – some ponies settle if they can look around from the safety of the horsebox, and some need walking around in hand. Others may benefit from lungeing in a quiet corner of the showground. Allow time to walk the course properly!

If the practice fence in the collecting ring is too high for warming up, make it lower. Build up gradually in height and width to something a little bigger than the jumps in the ring.

Avoid over-jumping the practice fence – only do enough to get your pony attentive, active and calm. Pop over the jump once or twice just before you go into the ring. Concentrate to the very last fence, and if your warming up and schooling routines are right for your pony, you should jump a clear round.

◄ **Arrive at a show** in plenty of time so your pony has time to settle in the exciting atmosphere. Give him a hay net while you take off his bandages and other travelling gear, then smarten him up and put the tack on.

▼ **By the time** of your first competition you should know your pony's ideal warm-up time. Try to find somewhere quiet to work so that, as well as being physically prepared, your pony is calm and listening to your aids.

Jumping a course

The golden rule for jumping a course successfully is 'think ahead'. If you know where you are going, plan your turns, ride straight and think about how you'll cope with each fence, then all should go well.

Related distances

A good course builder puts his fences at precise distances. He works out the striding between fences to suit the average pony in each class. When there is only room for up to five strides, the distance is 'related'.

Every pony has his own length of stride, so it is up to you to find out just how much ground your pony covers with each 'bound' of canter. Then you can decide how many strides he should take between two fences and how long they should be.

When working at home, spend some time counting your strides as you approach each fence. To start with, avoid altering your pony's stride to 'place' him correctly for take off. Keep him active, straight and balanced, counting 3-2-1 before he jumps. You should soon find that you are either pushing him on, or collecting him, to fit his strides to your count down.

Seeing a stride

Slowly, your eye becomes 'tuned' to your pony's stride. You begin to know how many strides you have to go and whether or not you should be lengthening or shortening for a good take off. This is called 'seeing a stride'. Ponies also learn to see a stride for themselves.

With practice, you will know the best approach for each fence, too. For example, the take-off point for a staircase is much closer than for a parallel. An upright needs more 'collection' – a shorter, more bouncy stride.

▼ **Most competitions** include either a double or a treble in the course. Some even have both. When jumping combinations, remember to approach the fences in a straight line and look at the centre of the furthest element. Keep a firm contact with the reins and push the pony on with your legs between each fence.

The right approach

When you walk a course, plan where you are going to make a turn so that your approach is the right length and straight. If your approach is too long, it is harder to count the stride; if it's too short, you won't see a stride in time, and could risk a refusal.

If your pony rushes, it may help to keep your approaches short. If you give him a long run-in to each fence, he could build up his speed and then flatten over the jump. A slower pony may need more room to build up his stride, particularly for wide spreads.

Straightness is essential, particularly through doubles and trebles as there is no room to correct a mistake. Ride for the centre of the furthest element of a combination. If you look only at the first part, you may meet the second fence crooked.

As you walk the course look for a point beyond each difficult fence to ride toward. This could be anything which will still be there when you enter the ring, like a tree.

Canter leads

When you turn, make sure that your pony is on the correct leg in canter. It's important to recognize if the pony is on the correct lead, so spend time at home practising canter work. A wrong lead leaves your pony unbalanced and can even bring about a fall. There are three ways to tackle this problem.

The easiest method (especially for a novice pony) is to return to trot and start again with the correct lead. Unfortunately this loses you valuable time.

Another way is to teach your pony to land after each fence with the lead you need for the next turn. This needs only a slight change in your own balance. While you are still in the air look in the direction you want to go. Then turn your body

slightly as well. This should be enough to tell your pony which lead he needs.

The third method is the 'flying change', where the pony changes his lead while remaining in canter. Some ponies do this naturally. You should only try a flying change with the help of a professional as the pony could easily canter 'disunited'. This means a pony changes in front only, so he leads with one leg in front and another behind. If your pony canters like this he'll be unbalanced and uncomfortable to ride.

Riding a course at home

You can build any number of courses at home to practise your jumping. Keep the fences fairly small and concentrate on maintaining an even rhythm throughout the course. Vary the fences from time to time and alter their positions regularly. Ponies have very good memories and they quickly learn a course!

Here's an example of a course you could build at home. Ride with determination toward fence 1. Keep your pony straight for fence 2 and look ahead. Collect him after fence 2 and turn slightly to meet fence 3 straight. It's an upright, so he needs a bouncy stride to jump it well.

After fence 4 look toward the double and start to turn gradually. Keep him straight through the double. Look to the left as you jump the second element to encourage him to land on the correct lead. Give yourself plenty of room to turn and approach fence 6 in a straight line.

Ride on as you approach fence 7 because you are riding away from home, and your pony may be reluctant. Ride straight between fences 7 and 8. When you land, look to the treble and begin to turn. Keep the pace steady and look at the centre of the third element. Keep him straight as you ride through the jumps and ride for home!

The course explained

Fence 1 is a simple spread.
Fence 2 is a parallel with rustic poles.
Fence 3 is a gate.
Fence 4 is another spread.
Fence 5a is a pole resting on some tyres.
Fence 5b is a spread.
Fence 6 is a hogs back.
Fence 7 is an upright with brush to fill it.
Fence 8 is a parallel using planks.
Fence 9a is a cross-poles.
Fence 9b is a parallel.
Fence 9c is a staircase using blocks.

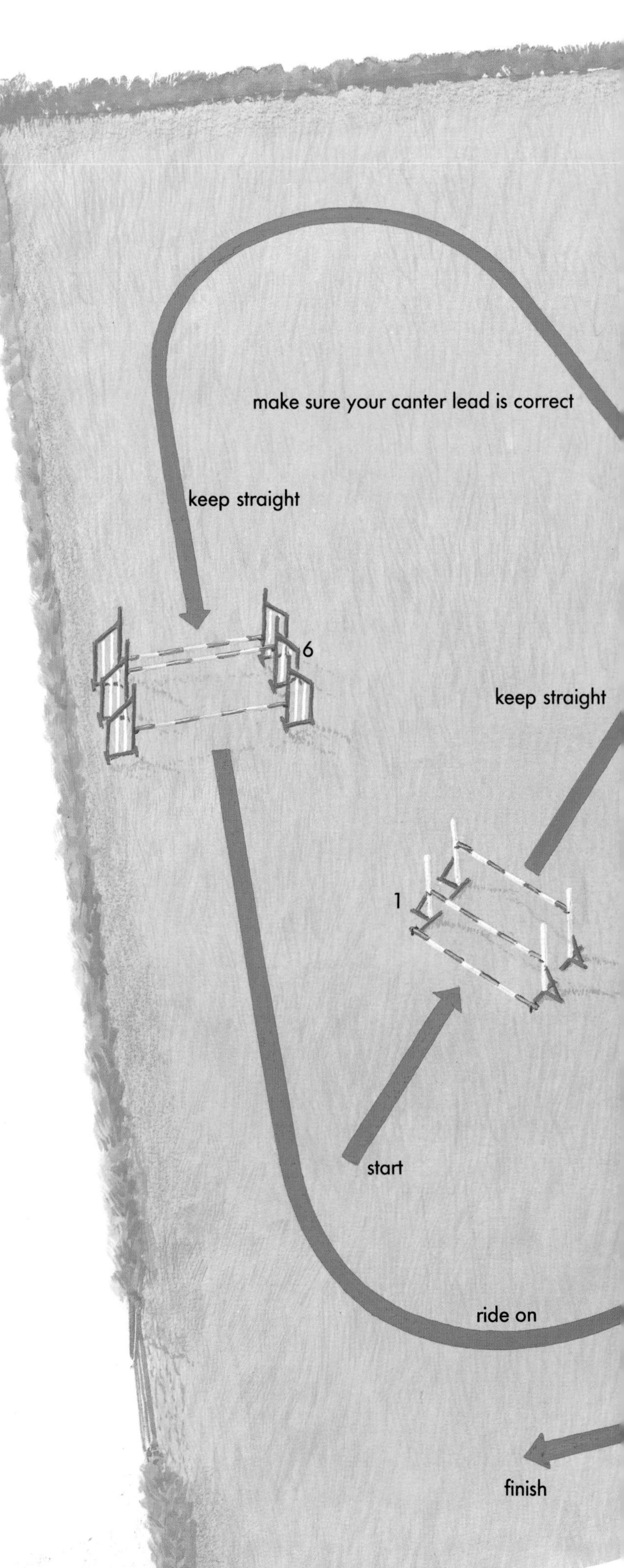

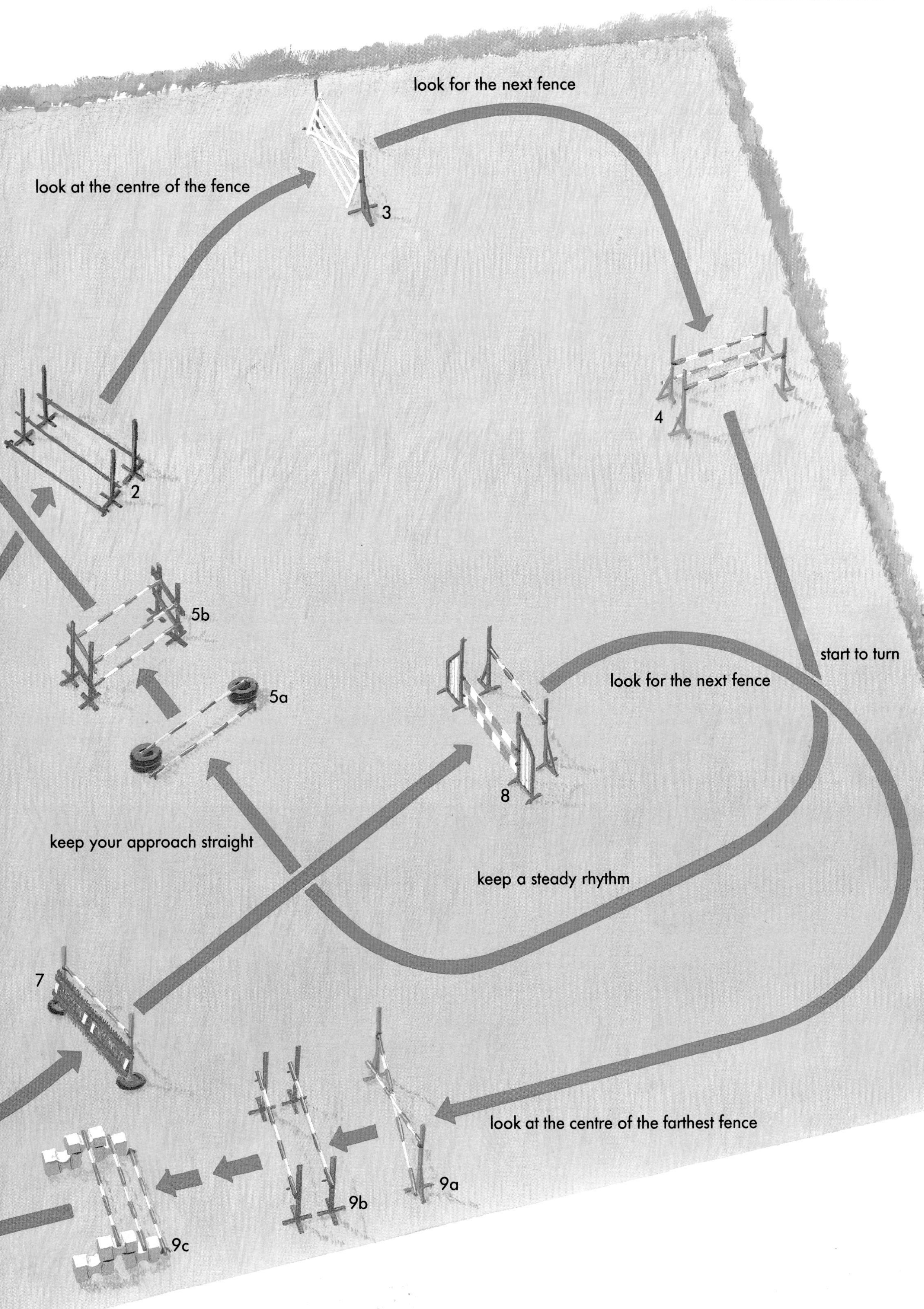
look for the next fence
look at the centre of the fence
3
4
2
5b
start to turn
look for the next fence
5a
8
keep your approach straight
keep a steady rhythm
7
look at the centre of the farthest fence
9a
9b
9c

Preparing for your first show can be so exciting that it's all too easy to forget something important. Once you have established a routine, you become more relaxed about the whole affair – and more efficient.

Advance warning

At least a week before the show, organize transport if you need it. Make sure that your driver is available and that the lorry or trailer is safe, serviced and fuelled. Breaking down on the way is the last thing you want!

Make a list of everything you need for the day, including the following:

- Saddle with girth and stirrups.
- Bridle and headcollar with a couple of strong ropes.
- Spare girths and stirrup leathers in case of breakages.
- A numnah if you use one.
- Overreach boots and brushing boots if your pony needs them.
- Full grooming kit plus plaiting kit for repairing plaits or taking them out.
- Studs if your pony has stud holes in his shoes.
- Your riding clothes – hat (and hairnet for girls), jacket, shirt, jodhpurs, tie, tie pin, gloves, whip and boots.
- Waterproof clothing and something cool to change into after your class.
- Money and refreshments.
- First-aid kit for you and your pony.
- Anti-sweat sheet and spare rugs.
- Water, buckets, hay nets and a feed for your pony.
- A copy of the schedule and a map of how to find the show ground.

You may add to this list or leave something out, but once you know exactly what you need, make several copies so that you can use it for reference every time you go to a show.

Take your time

Work out a timetable. If you know roughly what time your class starts, work backward from this.

If you plait the mane the night before, you'll have more time to feed, muck out, groom, bandage and load up before you leave home. Plaits done in the morning look smarter, however, and it's more comfortable for the pony to be plaited in the morning.

Give yourself plenty of time for the journey. If you think it is going to take 45 minutes, leave an hour to spare – the driver may lose the way or break down. Even if you hack to the show, leave time for possible delays.

Allow at least an hour for finding your way around the showground. You need time to collect your number, tack up your pony and ride him in. If your class starts at 11am, aim to be there by 10am *at the very latest!*

When you arrive, check that your ►

▼ **When you walk the course,** think about the best route to follow with your pony. Judge the distances between fences to see how many strides your pony needs to take. Look out for 'bogey' fences which may need more determined riding.

Professional riders plan their courses carefully. They look ahead to the next jump and know exactly where their horses are going to take off and how many strides they take between each fence.

►**Give your pony** a few practice jumps before you enter the ring. Ask a friend to help you by adjusting the height of the fence so you can concentrate on your jumping without having to dismount to alter the height.

pony is fresh and cool after the journey. Avoid giving him hay before competing. Put the ramp down so he can look out and see what's going on around him.

If you've hacked to the show, dismount and loosen the girths. Don't allow your pony to graze – if he eats grass, he'll be too full to jump properly and shower everywhere with green slobber!

Walking the course

Be on the alert and don't miss your chance to walk the course. When you do so, work out the track you'll take with your pony. Think about each fence and the problems it may have. Remember that jumping away from the collecting ring is more difficult and ponies often shorten their stride on the approach.

Every course has at least one 'spooky' fence that needs stronger riding. Look for any fences which your pony may need more encouragement to jump.

The last fence is often knocked down, especially if it is on the way to the collecting ring. Ride this one carefully, checking your pony before you jump to prevent him flattening over it.

Practice fences

After you've warmed up your pony and allowed him to have a look around the showground, give him a few practice jumps. Avoid over-exciting your pony, however, by jumping too much.

Start with small jumps and build up the size gradually. Some riders like to jump at least once over a fence a little bigger than those in the ring, so that when he competes, the pony finds the jumps well within his scope.

Look out for other riders practising at the same time and try to co-operate with them. There's nothing worse than putting the jump right down when somebody wants to jump higher fences.

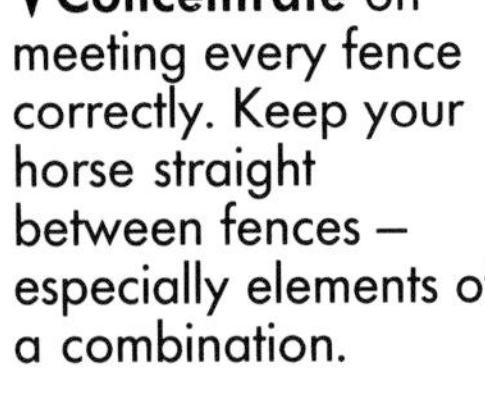

▼**Concentrate** on meeting every fence correctly. Keep your horse straight between fences – especially elements of a combination.

Jumping the course

If you're well prepared, you can really enjoy yourself. Stay calm and forget about the audience. Don't rush – ride every fence carefully and concentrate on meeting it correctly. If something goes wrong, put it behind you and think about the next jump.

If you make it to the jump off, the course may be altered and you could be asked to jump off against the clock. This does not mean galloping flat out! If you have a novice pony, go for a safe clear round. It's possible to cut corners without rushing.

Give your pony every chance to do his best. With experience, you can take more risks with short, fast approaches and jumping at an angle to save time.

Cooling down

When you've finished, reward your pony and walk him around on a loose rein to cool off. Offer him a small drink and put an anti-sweat rug on under his day rug for the journey home.

Don't expect too much if it's your first show. If your pony is looked after well this time, he is more likely to relax and enjoy many more shows.

▲**When your competition is over**, cool your pony down, take off his saddle and bridle and take out his plaits. He'll be glad to relax after all the excitement!

▼**If you prepare your pony properly** for a show, stay calm during the competition and look after him when it's over, he'll be happy to compete again.

Problem solver: refusals

Refusing is a shock for both you and your horse. Bring him back to basics to restore his confidence before competing again.

Ponies refuse jumps for all sorts of reasons. Some become frightened because they are asked to jump fences that are too high for them – this is especially true of young ponies. Others stop because their riders are nervous.

Patience and tact

If your pony *does* refuse his jumps, it's important to sort out the problem before it becomes worse. Patient schooling often cures the fault – bringing him back to trotting poles is one solution.

If the problem lies with you because you are rather nervous of jumping, some work on the lunge will improve your confidence and balance, and help you develop an independent seat.

If your pony still refuses, check your tack to make sure it doesn't pinch him.

Q

I have a young horse who seems frightened of jumping. He refuses every time I put him at a fence. What can I do to cure him?

A

Your horse was probably frightened at an early stage of his schooling. Young horses who show a talent for jumping can easily be 'overfaced', (asked to jump a fence too large for their ability).

Avoid jumping for a few weeks and concentrate on flatwork. When your horse is going freely forward from your leg, introduce some trotting poles. In one corner of your arena, place three or five trotting poles on a curve and trot over them. Allow your horse to stretch his head and neck forward so he can find his own way over the poles.

Once he is trotting happily over poles, introduce some low grids. Make the jumps as inviting as possible – use brush fences and low parallels to encourage your horse to jump.

The key to this kind of work is patience – you must take as much time as your horse needs to build up his confidence.

Q

I caught my pony in the mouth a few times when jumping and now he's starting to refuse fences. How can I persuade him to jump again?

A

Your pony has probably lost confidence in you. Ponies learn by association – if they do something that the rider wants they are petted and so encouraged to do as they are asked. They learn from bad experiences as well as good, so if you jab your pony when he jumps, he learns that jumping is painful and so stops.

The main reason you are jabbing the pony in the mouth is that you're using the bit to balance with. The only way to cure this fault is to develop an independent seat. This means that you move in harmony with the pony without using the reins to balance yourself.

Go to a good instructor for some lessons and advice. She might put you on the lunge for a few sessions as this is the best way for you to begin to develop your seat and ride independently.

During your training sessions at home you can improve your balance by riding without reins on the flat and over poles and grids.

Cantering with your upper body folded from the hips, in jumping position, is a good way to improve your balance. Keep your stirrups short to make it easier.

Once you have developed this independence, it is almost impossible to catch the pony in the mouth. Staying with him and allowing him to stretch his head and neck to balance himself become second nature.

Q

My horse often refuses at combination jumps. Could *my* nervousness of doubles be the reason?

A

Yes, novice riders often lose their nerve at doubles. Ponies can tell if their riders are nervous, and this makes *them* lose confidence. Many people feel such a sense of relief after the first part that they forget to ride forward to the next element!

To help you gain the confidence to push your pony on over fences, practise frequently over grids.

As you approach a combination, make sure you are straight. You should feel that the horse is taking you forward into the fence in balance and rhythm. Look at a point beyond the furthest element and ride positively toward it. Between the elements of a combination, pick your horse up quickly on landing, sit up and ride forward to the next jump.

Make sure the distances between the elements are right for your pony. Difficult distances could make the pony stop and shake your confidence in combinations.

If the problem occurs mainly at shows, remember that you need to ride more positively away from home as there are usually lots of distractions for your horse. Enter a class with fences lower than those you jump at home.

Q

My horse often puts in the odd stop for no apparent reason. Is he just playing up or is there another reason why he refuses?

A

When there's no obvious reason for a horse stopping, you have to look into less likely causes.

Check that no item of tack is pinching or that he has no sore places under the saddle. *Always* use a clean numnah under a sprung tree saddle to prevent the natural movement of the tree causing sores.

Look at your pony's mouth and check that he has no sharp edges on his teeth. He could be developing wolf teeth or other dental problems that would make a bit uncomfortable for him to wear.

Make all your jumps inviting. Fences with holes or no ground line can cause an inexperienced horse to stop. When you jump, *always* look at a point in the distance or your next fence. If you look into the bottom of the next fence you'll probably end up there!

Many horses 'try it on' occasionally for no particular reason – they need to be treated quite firmly. If your horse is still refusing after you have investigated all the possibilities, he may simply be playing up. Use your stick once, over his quarters as you reach the last stride before take-off point, and make sure you stay with him if he puts in a big jump!

Q

My horse seems reluctant to jump, particularly when the going is dry. Could the hard ground be hurting his legs, and what can I do about this?

A

Jumping, especially with a rider, often causes a horse to strain the tendons in his forelegs. This naturally makes him reluctant to jump. Bad shoeing can also make a horse stop.

Bear in mind that wet ground, too, can cause a strain because your horse has to pull his legs out of mud.

If you go to a competition and find that the ground is very hard, keep your practice jumps to a minimum. Pounding away on hard ground, or jumping out of heavy mud, won't do your horse's legs any good.

Jumping confidently on the day is just reward for all your hours of patient schooling.

Flatwork: pace variations

A true extended trot is beautiful to watch. The horse adopts a longer outline and lengthens his stride while keeping in perfect balance.

It's important to develop your horse's paces for all kinds of activities. Cross-country and show-jumping horses must lengthen and shorten their stride at a moment's notice to meet awkward fences correctly, while dressage horses must show the collected, medium and extended paces for advanced tests.

Feel the rhythm

When you school your horse, learn to feel what is happening underneath you. Is the horse rounding his back and accepting the bit, or is he raising his head and evading the bit?

By concentrating on what is going on under the saddle, you learn to recognize when your horse is going correctly, as well as what diagonal he's on in trot and what lead he takes in canter.

Once your horse is going forward quietly on the bit, you can introduce some variations of pace.

Lengthening the stride

It is easier to develop the lengthened stride before you try to achieve collection. The first time you ask your horse for a lengthened stride, try it in rising trot on the long side of the arena, or across the diagonal, after you have come out of a corner. The corner allows you to generate enough energy in the quarters to lengthen the stride. You create this impulsion with a series of half halts that collect your horse, attract his attention and warn him that you're going to do something different. Half halts also help you to balance him.

Avoid asking for too much lengthening to begin with as this can confuse your horse. In the early stages, it's easy to push the horse out of his stride and make him break into canter.

The aids to lengthen

To ask your horse for a longer stride, apply both legs evenly on the girth, brace your back and push down and forward with your seat. Allow the horse to adopt a longer, lower outline with your hands while maintaining contact and keeping him on the bit.

If your horse is lengthening properly he keeps a good rhythm, lowers his head a little and stretches his legs. You can clearly feel his back swinging from side to side through the saddle.

As your horse improves and lengthens his strides without losing rhythm or balance, you can ask him for medium trot. This is when the horse overtracks – his hindfeet touching the ground in front of

▼**Ask for lengthened** strides at all paces. In extended canter, the horse maintains a regular three-time rhythm and covers more ground than in working canter.

◄**Leg-yielding** is a helpful exercise for gaining your horse's attention and making him responsive to your aids.

▼**Ask your horse** for some strides in shoulder-in to prepare him for a lengthened stride. Shoulder-in engages the joints of the hindleg and makes it easier for the horse to go forward energetically into medium or extended trot.

the footprints of the forefeet.

In the extended trot, the horse covers as much ground as possible while remaining in balance. The extended paces are introduced to dressage tests at medium level. Every horse starts his training with a few lengthened strides and gradually builds up to medium and extended paces.

Collection

While the medium and extended paces are extravagant and impressive, the collected paces are beautiful because of the elevation of the steps. The passage and piaffe show this most dramatically.

The collected paces require as much energy as the lengthened ones. To shorten the stride, you engage the quarters by using your legs, as you do for lengthening. Your hands restrain and allow the horse alternately – this raises the forehand and produces a higher shorter step.

Ask your horse for collected trot on a circle. He must be relaxed and going forward freely from your leg – you cannot force him to collect his pace by resisting with your hands.

Helpful movements

Shoulder-in and leg-yielding can both be used to vary your schooling and prevent your horse becoming bored.

If you want to shorten your horse's stride and then lengthen it again, use a shoulder-in. By engaging all three joints of the hindleg, shoulder-in lightens the forehand and collects the horse. Ask for a few steps of shoulder-in when coming out of a corner, then send the horse forward across the diagonal of the arena. He should produce some energetic lengthened strides.

Leg-yielding on a circle is another good exercise for altering your horse's stride. Ask him to shorten his pace on the way into the circle and lengthen it on the way out. Leg-yielding helps to make your horse supple and responsive.

Canter work

You can lengthen your horse's canter in the same way as his trot. Concentrate on maintaining the regular three-time rhythm. Work on circles creating an even tempo and then ask for some lengthening of stride on the long side of the arena.

It's vital to keep the canter balanced as it's easy for the horse to lose his rhythm by falling into a fast trot after a lengthened canter.

Walk variations

The walk is the most difficult gait and is often neglected. To lengthen your horse's walk, keep an even contact with his mouth, count the four-time rhythm and push him forward using your legs alternately. He should keep a regular rhythm and overtrack.

At the collected walk the horse marches energetically with elevated steps. If you want a collected walk, work on small circles and use plenty of upward and downward transitions to keep him interested.

Pace and patience

The key to asking your horse to vary his paces is patience. Although some horses cannot extend fully because of poor conformation, all horses' paces can be developed to their own ability.

▼ **In piaffe,** the horse springs from one diagonal to the other demonstrating perfect balance and collection. A good piaffe must show impulsion and a regular rhythm to the trot.

Fitness plans for...

After six weeks of road work, trotting and gentle cantering, your horse should be half fit. A short, easy day's hunting should not be too much for him. A further 4-week fitness programme is needed to bring the horse to the condition required for eventing and hard hunting.

▼ **A well-balanced** and carefully planned fitness routine pays dividends on the cross-country course. If a horse has not been properly prepared for this strenuous exercise, he simply will not be able to cope.

All in a day's work

The horse needs to be fitter for a three-day event than he does for a one-day event. For horses that are aimed at three-day eventing, one-day horse trials can be used as stepping stones to peak performance fitness.

A horse going in for a novice one-day event or a day's hunting needs to be fit enough to take at least two hours' work. For an eventer this is split into three phases. He is ridden for almost 60 minutes in the dressage, up to 30 minutes in the show jumping and for another 30 minutes in the cross country – this includes a 5-minute gallop. The hunter has to stand up to a longer period of work: probably 3-5 hours. There is usually plenty of standing around time, however, between the bursts of fast work, to help him catch his breath.

Fit at any event

To build up fitness for eventing the horse's work load has to be increased gradually to avoid straining muscles or ligaments. Fast work should be done twice weekly, with two or three days reserved for rest. It is important to give

...eventing and hunting

him plenty of road work to harden up his limbs and tone his muscles.

A good hack is an enjoyable part of the programme. If you live in a hilly district, the hack can be shorter than in flat country. Work up to about two hours out as the horse gets fitter.

About 10 days before his first event, give your horse a good long canter. If he blows and is lazy, he should have another two canters of similar length before the event. A sharp and clean-winded horse needs only a short 'pipe opener', preferably up a hill.

A typical week's training would be:
Monday: 90 minutes road work.
Tuesday: No more than 45 minutes schooling, then about 30 minutes hack.
Wednesday: Introduce fast canter work.
Thursday: 20 minutes flat work in the school followed by a 60-minute hack.
Friday: Gridwork with some dressage, then a 45-minute hack.
Saturday: Fast work.
Sunday: A day of rest, but give him a walk in-hand or let him out in the field to stretch his legs.

Increasing the work load means stepping up the amount of work done within these periods of time, *not* spending more time at work.

If possible, turn your horse out in a paddock for about an hour every day, so that he can unwind, relax and generally do as he pleases. This gives a fit horse a chance to exercise himself and run off any excess energy, thus helping him to settle to dressage work.

Interval training

▲ **Interval training** is a cantering exercise that improves the horse's stamina without overstraining him. It is normally done at a faster canter and in the forward seat.

▲ **After 5 minutes** brisk cantering, slow to a walk for a minute. This

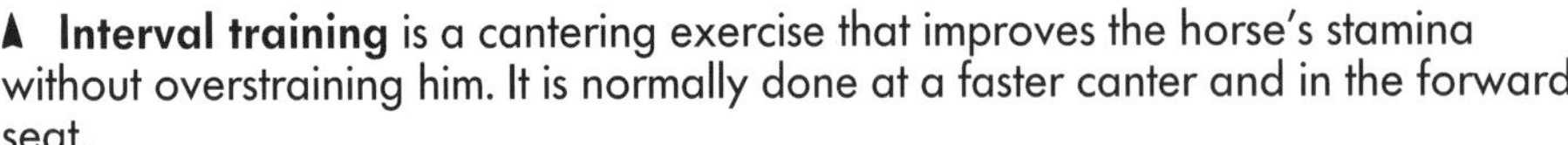

Take it easy

Bear in mind that an injury will cause a severe set-back in your horse's programme and that a serious injury means a lengthy rest. All fitness work has to be geared to improving stamina *without* putting undue strain on the horse. This is why road work, trotting and hill work are crucial, and very fast work is less important. Mad galloping invites injury and does little for the horse. For this reason, the cantering exercise of **interval training** is preferable to galloping when it comes to fast work.

Interval training means the horse has breaks in between bouts of cantering. These 'breathers' help him to recover slightly before setting off again. A horse in training, for example, may do three lots of 5-minute cantering, with two 1-minute intervals. This builds up fitness without putting too much strain on the horse's lungs, heart or legs.

Fitness not fizz

Feed your horse according to the amount of work he is doing, his temperament (fizzy or calm) and metabolic rate (how well he converts food into energy). You learn to gauge how much food a horse should be having only through experience: there are no strict rules on feeding for fitness. A fit eventer should look lean (but not thin) and carry no extra weight to slow him down.

As a horse gets fitter, his digestive system becomes more delicate. Avoid sudden changes in his daily meals, especially during the last week before a big event. As he becomes fitter, he eats less bulk food, so reduce his hay rations when he starts leaving some. Cut down feeds slightly on his rest day to prevent the risk of azoturia. A fit horse is more likely to contract this complaint than an unfit one.

Toward the final stages of his fitness programme, the horse should have four meals a day: early in the morning, at lunch-time, at the end of the day and later in the evening. He may become a slightly fussy eater, so tempt him with treats in his feed: carrots and molasses usually do the trick. If you are in any doubt about feeding, seek advice from an experienced person.

It's impossible to lay down hard and fast rules for precise fitness routines. Each horse is an individual and needs different work as a result. The type of horse, his temperament and character all have to be considered before the final details of a fitness programme are established. You'll know when you've hit upon a suitable routine for your horse – his condition will tell you.

gives the horse the opportunity to catch his breath.

▲ **Break into** a canter again. By this time, the horse feels the benefit of his short breather and is ready to increase the pace.

Fit for hunting

Stamina and fitness are important qualities for the hunter as well as the eventer. The difference is that a hunter has to have even more staying power. The horse is often out for up to 5 hours when hunting and, although he may have breaks in between cantering and galloping about, there are times when he may be on the go all day long.

You can prepare a hunter for this kind of work by hacking – with progressively longer and more demanding work on the roads – up to 2½ hours. If there are plenty of hills to climb, then the odd trot up them is a good idea. If the country is flat, increase the trotting until, after about eight weeks work, it makes up half the exercise time.

A very short day's hunting after 6–8 weeks is a good way of getting a horse fitter for hard hunting.

2: Mounted Games

The fun of mounted games

There are hundreds of horseback games to choose from – but it is the same two ingredients that make them such fun. They improve your riding, and they give you the chance to pit your skills against friends!

Riding skills

Most mounted games have simple rules and only a few essential props. The real challenge lies in stretching your riding ability to the full and in learning new ways of improving on what you know.

You must keep control of your pony and finish your turn in the games as fast as you can. Holding the reins in either hand, mounting and dismounting from either side, vaulting on or off when your pony is moving, changing pace or direction smoothly – with all these skills you'll be a difficult competitor to beat!

Organizing games

The summer holidays are the best time for organizing group activities. Because the ground is dry, there's less danger of slipping over than in a muddy field. And you'll have more opportunity to practise with the fine, light evenings.

At first practise for short periods

▼ **Games** on horseback are not just competitive – they also test a wide range of riding skills. In the Groom's race below, for example, you must know how to lead a pony properly and be able to complete your turn speedily. Here, the competitor has her feet out of the stirrups to save vital seconds when she dismounts.

because some games can be quite tiring. Get your pony used to things gradually. If you spend all day galloping around on a pony that's never done more than gentle hacking, you'll exhaust him!

Aim to pit riders of the same ability against each other. That way everyone can find their own level and enjoy the competitive element of the games.

If you find the prospect of organizing games yourself a bit daunting, ask the advice of an experienced rider – ideally a qualified instructor. It's important that the props you use are safe and that neither ponies nor riders overdo it.

Taking games further

If you enjoy mounted games with friends, there are several ways to extend your skills. Your local riding school may well hold gymkhanas in the summer, where a variety of races and competitive games are played.

If you have your own pony you can also join the Pony Club. It holds rallies and gymkhanas and organizes summer camps for about a week each year. You can take your pony with you and learn to ride with professional instruction – while enjoying a holiday break at the same time.

WINNING WAYS

Practise mounted games at a walk or trot before attempting to gallop. Both you and your pony need to learn the game thoroughly.

Don't be over ambitious at first. Only attempt games which you can tackle confidently.

Never use a whip. It gets in the way and shows you're not in control. The use of a whip is banned by the Pony Club.

Even when not on horseback, everyone taking part must wear hard hats. Remember, safety first.

To increase your speed, practise mounting from either side and using either hand on the reins.

Make sure there's an experienced rider around to help out.

Ride without your stirrups so that you can get on and off your pony quickly.

Think of your pony – don't overdo it!

Practice makes perfect

When choosing team games, think about how many riders are involved and what kind of props you need. Games like the ball and cone race (opposite) have very simple props and can be played by just two riders, if you haven't enough competitors to make up two teams. The fishing race (right) needs lots of equipment and is best with at least ten players.

THE FISHING RACE
This is a game for at least two teams of five (four riders and one non-rider). Each team needs a bin containing four wooden, aluminium or plastic fish, a 'fishing rod' and a T-shaped wooden stand to hang the fish on.

1

1 Four team members have to ride, one at a time, from the starting line to the bin, hook out a fish with the 'fishing rod' and gallop to the post at the change-over line.

2

2 If a rider drops a fish he can pick it up while mounted or, if it's easier, he can dismount, pick it up and continue.

The fifth member waits at the change-over line, unhooks the fish from the rider's fishing rod and hangs it on the cross-piece. The rider has to stay behind the line until the fish is correctly placed on the hook.

3

3 The rider then gallops to the starting line and hands the 'fishing rod' to the second team member, who follows the same routine.

The winning team is the one whose last member crosses the finishing line first – with all four fish on the stand.

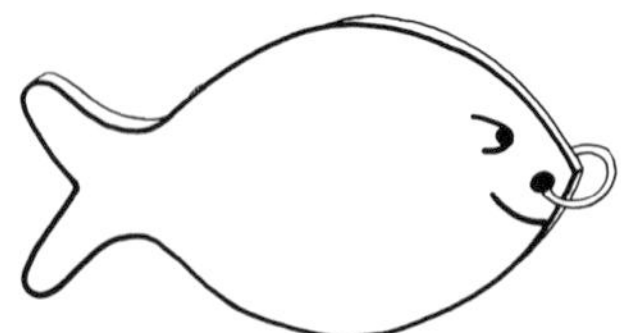

EQUIPMENT NEEDED
☐ 2 bins 45-75cm (18-30in) high, with a 30-45cm (12-18in) mouth.
☐ 8 fish 35-40cm (15-16in) long and 18-20cm (7-8in) across. Each fish has a 2cm (1in) ring through its nose.
☐ 2 T-shaped stands, 120cm (4ft) tall with a 90cm (2ft) cross-piece.
☐ 8 large cup hooks. Screw 4 hooks, equally spaced, on to the underside of each stand.
☐ 2 rods, each 120cm (4ft) long. Screw a cup hook into the end of each rod and tape it securely into place.

BALL AND CONE RACE

This is a team game for four people on each side. Two cones are placed in a line. The second one has a tennis ball on top.

The lead rider gallops up to the first cone carrying a tennis ball which must be placed on top of the cone. The rider then gallops on to the second cone, collects the ball from it and takes it back to the second competitor waiting at the change-over line.

The second rider completes his turn in the same way. The team whose fourth rider crosses the finishing line carrying a ball is the winner.

If a cone is knocked over or a ball is dropped the rider should dismount and correct the mistake. Dismount as quickly as possible so that you don't lose too much time (above left) and carefully place the tennis ball in position (above right). With practice you can control your horse and improve your balance giving you the perfect position (below).

Mounted games know-how

A wide variety of games is played at mounted games competitions: some have been firm favourites for years, but new ones are being invented all the time.

Know the rules

It is obviously important to know the rules for each individual game inside out. However, make sure, too, that you are fully familiar with the general rules which apply to every event.

One seemingly simple mistake could mean elimination for your whole team – for example, crossing the change-over line too soon, or passing the wrong side of a bending post. You *are* allowed to go back and correct your mistakes, provided you have not left the arena and the game is still in progress.

You are also allowed – and are eliminated if you don't – to re-assemble props that you knock over (such as containers and posts), and to dismount and retrieve items that you drop.

If you fall during a race you have to remount and resume the race from the exact place where you fell. If you are thought to be riding dangerously or behaving badly you may be disqualified.

★ **STARTER'S ORDERS**
The starting signal for a race is the drop of a flag. If the starter thinks the start was unfair, he raises the flag again and recalls the riders by blowing a whistle. Try to assist him by keeping your pony steady (but ready!) behind the starting line. You may be ordered to stand behind the other ponies if your own pony gets too excited.

The stepping stone dash

◄ Six stepping stones (tubs or tins) for each team are placed across the centre line of the arena, in a straight line up and down. Two team members are mounted at the start end of the arena, and the other two at the opposite end. When the starting signal is given, Number 1 gallops to the stepping stones, dismounts and runs across them leading her pony (by the rein nearest to her). She remounts from the ground after the last 'stone', and gallops to the change-over line. Numbers 2, 3 and 4 repeat the process in succession. The winning team is the one whose Number 4 is first across the finishing line. If you knock a stone over, or if your foot touches the ground while crossing the stones, you must go back and cross the whole line again.

Balloon bursting

▼ Six balloons are anchored to the ground on the centre line of the arena, in a straight line up and down. The four team members are mounted, two at each end of the arena. Number 1 holds a lance, which is usually a cane with a drawing pin attached to the end. On the start signal, Number 1 gallops to the end of the arena, bursting a balloon on the way, and hands the lance to Number 2. The remaining three team members repeat the process, each bursting a balloon on their way up or down the arena. The winners are the team whose Number 4 crosses the finish line first, carrying the lance. You are allowed to have more than one attempt at bursting a balloon, but if you fail the whole team is eliminated. There is no penalty if you burst more than one balloon.

▼ **Bring your own** team supporters to cheer you on – as long as they don't try to help you in any way!

The five flag race

For each team, flag holders (open-topped cones) are placed on the centre line and behind the change-over line. Each team has five flags on canes, four in the holder on the centre line, and one carried by Number 1 at the start. On the starting signal, Number 1 gallops to the end of the arena and places the flag in her team's holder. She then gallops back, picks a second flag out of the holder on the centre line, and hands this to Number 2 at the start line. Numbers 2, 3 and 4 repeat the process in succession, so that at the end of the game the team has placed four flags in the holder at the change-over line, and Number 4 finishes by crossing the start line carrying the fifth flag. If you accidentally take more than one flag from the holder you must replace the surplus, and if you knock the holder over you have to dismount, pick it up and replace the flags.

The potato race

A

For each team four potatoes are placed behind the change-over line, on the ground with a ring marked round them so you can see them. A bucket is placed on the centre line for each team. When the signal to start is given Number 1, carrying a potato, gallops to his team's bucket and drops the potato into it (**A**), steadying his pony while he aims.

If the potato misses the bucket, the rider has to dismount, pick it up and place it in the bucket (**B**), then remount. He then continues to the change-over line (but doesn't actually have to cross it), dismounts, picks up a second potato

B

Nine ring race

A bending pole with a hook on it (facing the start line) is placed on the centre line for each team. Team member Number 5 is on the change-over line holding a T-shaped stand. This has four hooks on it, on each of which are placed two small white or coloured rings. Number 1 starts with a ring, and on the signal rides to the centre line and places the ring on the bending pole hook. She continues to the change-over line and collects two more rings from the stand. She returns to the centre line, hangs one of the rings on the hook, then rides back to the start line and passes the second ring to Number 2. Numbers 2 and 3 repeat the process in exactly the same way, but Number 4 has to leave both rings on the centre hook before riding across the finish line. The winners are the team whose Number 4 finishes first, and with all nine rings correctly placed on the centre hook.

C

and remounts (**C**) – with the potato in his mouth if he wishes! While dismounted, you have to keep hold of the pony by the rein at all times.

He rides as fast as he can back to the start line (**D**). To save valuable seconds this competitor has not retrieved his stirrups for the return journey! At the line he hands the potato over to Number 2. Numbers 2, 3 and 4 repeat the process in succession, except that Number 4 drops the last potato into the bucket on his way back to the finish. The winners are the team whose Number 4 is first across the finishing line.

D

Mounted games: training

▼ **The team parade:** This moment of pride is the reward for a thorough training programme.

The key to success in mounted games is plenty of practice. Your pony must be agile and obedient to understand what is required of him in the high-speed excitement of the games. You and the pony must also have confidence in each other, so the more riding you do together the better.

Spoken commands

Obedience to the voice is an asset not only in mounted games but in many aspects of horse management. First your pony should obey the word *stand* spoken clearly but quietly every time you mount, stop, tie him up or hold him to wait. *Walk on, trot, canter, back, over* (sideways movement) and *up* (moving toward something), spoken with the appropriate natural aids, can be introduced gradually. Lungeing is very useful when training the pony to obey your voice.

Always reward your pony when he gives the correct response. Even when you are quite capable of vaulting on at a gallop, standing still at your command is very important. It is vital for such activities as opening gates, and throwing objects into or fishing them out of buckets, as many games require.

Leading

Teach your pony to follow readily when you are leading him, even if you are ➤

★ **YOUR MOUNT**

When choosing a pony for mounted games it is better to select one on the small side. This makes vaulting easier, and small ponies are usually handier at manoeuvring quickly.

The pony should not be nervous and excitable, or he will get out of hand in the turmoil of games. But equally he should not be dull and stupid – he needs to be quick-thinking and learn to anticipate his rider's actions.

He should be over five years old, because the rough-and-tumble of mounted games is harsh on a young animal's soft mouth and bones.

➤ **Your pony must become familiar** with strange objects such as balloons, sacks and flags (just as a police horse has to!). Include as many different items as you can in your training programme.

▲ **Persuading your pony** to leave his friends behind takes time.

► **Teach your pony** to stand still while you collect objects from poles and buckets. This coloured coat helps to get the pony used to objects flapping near his head.

▼ **Practise techniques** such as passing objects to each other before you have to do it for 'real'. This also ensures your pony has time to learn what to do.

hopping along in a sack. You should lead him firmly without tugging or looking back at him. Normally when you lead a pony, you take the reins over his head and hold both together under his chin with your right hand, and the loop of the reins in your left.

However, this is not always possible in mounted games where speed is all-important. When they are round the pony's neck, try to hold both reins close to his head rather than pulling hard on one side – this can result in pulling the bit right through the mouth.

As well as following you, your pony must get used to being led from another pony, and standing still while held by another rider. Practise both with a friend. Be gentle in all your handling of ponies: it is the ones who have been jagged in the mouth and pulled about who become difficult.

Suppling exercises

Suppleness is important in all riding, but especially in mounted games where the pony has to bend and turn at speed. Many horses have a natural tendency to favour one side, which means they bend more easily and fluently one way than the other. Lungeing is a good exercise to help overcome this problem and develop suppleness.

In your schooling sessions, do circling work once a week with more emphasis on the stiffer side. Combine this with bending practice, starting in trot and increasing your speed gradually until you can bend in and out of the posts at a gallop.

Practice sessions intended to improve

suppleness should be carried out at a trot or steady canter. Only gallop when you are practising a specific game and, even then, start every new exercise at a slow pace and speed up gradually.

Group practice

Practise vaulting, riding without stirrups, opening and closing gates, and lowering and replacing slip rails. Also get used to collecting, carrying and throwing objects, and passing them to other riders.

Some practice can be carried out alone, but working with others is essential. It teaches ponies to be obedient in company. Many only agree to hurry when they are joining their friends, and are unwilling to move when asked to leave them. They must also learn to wait while the others gallop off in their turn.

If, at any point in his training, your pony gets out of hand and upset, stop the lesson at once and forget about it until the next day. Rushing things too fast is the most likely cause of bad temper and muddling. Specific exercises should last no longer than 15 minutes about three times a week. Vary the exercises to prevent boredom, and ideally combine them with hacking out so the pony stays keen and alert.

▼ MUG RACE
For five players you need five mugs. Place four mugs on a table at one end of a line of bending posts. The first player holds the fifth mug, gallops to the first post and hangs the mug on top. The player collects another mug from the table and carries it back to the second rider who repeats the pattern, and so on, until each mug is hanging on a post. Any mugs knocked off must be replaced before the game continues.

▲ ROPE RACE
Two riders wait at each end of a row of posts. The first player, carrying a 60cm (24in) length of rope, bends in and out of the posts, and gives the second player one end of the rope. They bend back, linked together, to the third rider, who swaps places with the first. Alternating pairs bend along the row until all players have taken part – this team has made it trickier by leaving the mugs out from the last race!

Mounted games: neck reining

Turning at high speed is an extra skill needed by pony and rider in mounted games – made even more tricky when you are holding the reins in one hand, and carrying a prop for the game in the other.

Riding one-handed

Activities which need the reins to be held in one hand – such as mounted games, Western riding and polo – mean the pony is guided by neck reining.

As the name implies, neck reining means you put pressure on the *neck*, as well as on the mouth. You apply the usual leg aids, combined with pressure of the rein on the opposite side of the pony's neck from the turn.

To direct the pony your legs always move before your hands. He must learn to move away from pressure of your lower leg behind the girth. The rein hand is then moved with a *small* wrist movement into the turn. An over-strong movement turns the pony's head *against* the direction in which he is moving.

Holding the reins

To ride with both reins in the left hand, take the right rein between the first and second finger (or the first finger and thumb), with the slack passing across the palm, and the left rein between the third and little finger with the slack rein

HOLDING THE REINS

There are various ways of holding your reins in one hand, and you soon find the arrangement you feel most comfortable with.

This is one method, with the reins in the right hand. Take the left rein between the first finger and thumb, with the slack passing across the palm. Pass the right rein between the third and little finger with the slack crossing the palm in the opposite direction.

Which hand you hold the reins in depends on the game and what you have to do. For example, if you are leading another pony on the left, your reins have to be in your right hand. But if you have to pick up a prop such as a mug or potato, your reins have to be in your left hand (if you are right-handed).

➤ **The skill of** neck reining is called for in virtually every mounted game.

crossing the palm in the opposite direction.

Hold the left hand palm down, so you see the back of it when you look down. Keep your wrist slightly curved – it must be supple with gentle flexing, not sharply angled.

If you are left handed, reverse the instructions. The aim is to leave your stronger hand free to carry out whatever activity the game involves. It is useful, however, to be able to control your pony confidently with either hand.

Handle with care

It's hard to avoid pulling on the pony's mouth when making hasty checks and turns in mounted games. But you should reduce this stress as much as possible by handling him carefully, and remembering just how painful a jerk in the mouth is for him.

The bit lies on the bars of the mouth, which are very sensitive due to the concentration of nerve endings under the skin. If these are destroyed by rough handling the pony becomes hard-

▼ **Keeping your own** and your partner's pony steady while she vaults on is not easy – the ponies know their next move is to gallop off!

mouthed and difficult to control. Use only a simple snaffle bit: a thick vulcanite one is kinder than the usual nickel or stainless steel when taking part in hectic activities.

It might be useful to fit your pony with a standing martingale. This helps to prevent the pony from resisting by throwing his head about. And, if you lose your balance, the neck strap provides a useful grab-hold rather than hanging on to the reins.

Practising turns

As with all new exercises, first practise neck reining slowly in walk. Guide your pony with your legs and by neck reining in a series of turns of gradually increasing sharpness up to the full 360° 'about turn'. This is known as 'turning on a sixpence'.

Increase the speed gradually to trot then canter. Keep individual lessons short – never more than 15-20 minutes in a single session.

Ball and racket race

This is a game for four team members, and any number of teams. It tests the rider's skill at guiding the pony by neck reining and making carefully balanced turns.

EQUIPMENT
For each team you need:
- ☐ Tennis racket.
- ☐ Tennis ball.
- ☐ Four bending posts.

1 The first team member balances a ball on a tennis racket, and on the starting signal proceeds to bend in and out of a row of bending posts. She keeps the pony steady and has her eyes on the ball all the time.

2 The ball must not be touched by hand except if you drop it. Then, you have to dismount, pick it up, remount, replace it on the racket and continue. The rider has finished bending and is heading back to'the line.

Tyre race

Again, this game has four team members and any number of teams. This game tests the riders' skills in dismounting and vaulting on at speed, leading another pony while riding their own, and making a very quick turn-round at the end of the arena.

EQUIPMENT
For each team you need:
- ☐ A lightweight, thin-rimmed tyre.

1 Two team members gallop up to the mid-line where a tyre has been placed. Just before they reach the line, one rider jumps off and runs toward the tyre, while her partner takes her pony's reins.

2 The rider on the ground steps into the tyre, picks it up and threads it over her body so she has gone completely 'through' it. Meanwhile her partner carries on going with the two ponies to save vital seconds.

Always keep the pony well balanced and leading with the correct inside leg – which changes with each change of direction – otherwise he could cross his legs at speed and fall over. You may find your pony helps you here by performing natural 'flying changes': changing the leading leg at speed without coming back to trot.

Another method of turning sharply is for your pony to make a 'turn on the haunches', pivoting round his inside hindleg. Ask him to make even, quiet steps with his forelegs round his inner hindfoot, using pressure with your outside leg well behind the girth and with the outside rein against his neck.

Again, practise this movement at increasing speed, keeping your instructions to the pony very clear. When you are confident that your pony understands what you are asking him to do, put the movements into practice in some games.

3 Back at the starting line, the first rider hands the racket-with-ball to the second rider. This is the trickiest part – here the ball has fallen during the change-over. The first rider is dismounting to pick it up so that the second team member can get started.

4 She places the ball back on the racket, and the second rider repeats the process of bending up and down the poles, and so on until all team members have taken their turn. The winners are the team whose fourth member crosses the finish line first *with the ball on the racket!*

3 She runs to catch up with her partner and gets back on her pony. More time is saved here if you are able to vault on. The two riders gallop to the end of the line as fast as they can, where the third team member is waiting for them.

4 At the line, the second rider (who didn't go through the tyre) turns quickly to go back down the line with the third rider. It is the second rider who goes through the tyre this time. The game continues until each team member has gone through the tyre. The fastest team wins.

76

3: Dressage

Practising the square halt

Introduction to dressage

The word dressage simply means training a riding horse. Any pony can be taught obedience and balanced movement if you ride it thoughtfully and carefully – which is what dressage is all about.

The aims of dressage

The object of training the riding horse is the same as for any athlete or dancer. Circuit and weight training in the gymnasium do for the long-distance runner what dressage does for the horse – they make him strong, supple and agile, and improve his co-ordination.

All well-schooled horses go through a period of dressage training. It is essential for success and enjoyment in all kinds of riding – jumping, gymkhanas, polo, cross country and hacking. By teaching your pony properly you'll help him to stay sound and healthy, gallop faster, turn more quickly, jump higher, be safer and more obedient.

It is a rewarding challenge to train a horse well. But first you need to know a little about the horse's movement in his natural state. Only then can you perfect his paces despite the weight of a rider.

First steps in dressage

The horse is a naturally graceful and swift animal. But when you sit on his back to ride him, you upset his balance and limit the range of his natural paces.

To reduce or, preferably, remove any discomfort – some horses' feet and legs suffer; others get back pain from the rider's weight – you must sit correctly, giving the horse an evenly balanced load to carry. This is one of the reasons why riding instructors pay so much attention to your position in the saddle.

Once you've established a good seat you can aim to improve your pony's natural paces and outline while carrying a rider. Training a horse to perform the walk, trot and canter well is the basis for all dressage training.

Practising your paces

At any pace, your pony should move forward energetically and willingly with a good rhythm. He should be relaxed and looking ahead at all times. Unless going in a straight line, he should be flexed a little to the direction in which he is going. He must be calm and put up no resistance, and be alert to your instructions.

You need to practise the three main paces – walk, trot and canter – until your pony maintains both his balance and rhythm at any speed – and until you do, too! All transitions, particularly trot to canter and back again, should be smooth, calm and quiet.

Study closely how the horse moves. Think about what he is actually doing. Riding becomes really fascinating when

◄ **Practising the square halt** is one of the first steps in training a pony in dressage. A horse should stand still on all four legs with his weight evenly distributed. Always keep contact with your pony's mouth so that he is alert to your instructions.

◄ **This is a perfectly square halt** – note that the pair of forelegs and the pair of hindlegs are parallel.

A dressage arena

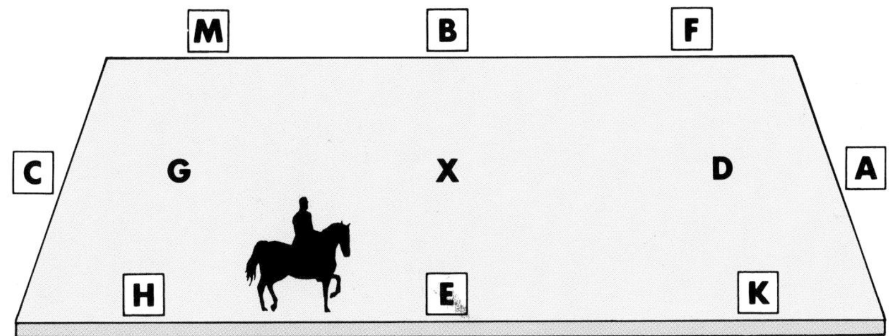

A basic dressage arena measures 20 metres (66ft) wide and 40 metres (132ft) long. Letters are used as markers around the edge and across the middle of the arena. These are traditional and act as points of reference. They have no special meaning.

In a dressage test you and your pony have to perform particular movements that start and finish at a given letter. The examiners test your ability to ask the pony to perform various steps. They also test your pony's understanding and obedience.

To get used to a dressage arena, start by practising smooth transitions from walk to trot and trot to canter as you reach your chosen letter.

The same arena and letters are used for most tests up to elementary level. After that, a longer arena (60 metres/198ft) with more letters is used more often.

LEARNING THE LETTERS

One of the easiest ways of remembering the position of the letters round a dressage arena is by learning a rhyme.

Try to memorize a phrase like All King Edward's Horses Carry Many Brave Fighters.

The first letter of each word indicates a letter in the dressage arena. This way you'll know the letters off-by-heart in no time at all.

you understand your pony's stride pattern and you know how to influence this. Each pace has a different action and alters the appearance of the horse.

The walk is a four-time movement in which the horse has three hooves on the ground at any one time. But there's more to it than that. The head and neck swing up and down in rhythm with the stride. To show that he is relaxed and supple your pony's tail should swing softly. The walk must be purposeful. Ideally, your pony looks as though he is off to keep an important appointment: he is not in a hurry and has plenty of time, but he is making sure that he won't be late.

The trot: It is easy to feel, when rising at the trot, that your pony trots in two-time. He should spring lightly along, jumping from one diagonal pair of feet to the other, with a moment of suspension in between when none of his feet are on the ground.

The canter should be a light, swinging pace in which the horse uses his whole body in a soft, relaxed way, nodding his head and neck in rhythm with the stride.

It is a three-time movement – either hindleg lifts and is followed by the other hindleg with its diagonal foreleg and finally the other foreleg. This foreleg is known as the leading leg. If you are cantering to the right, this remaining foreleg should be the right one. If you are cantering to the left, the left foreleg must lead.

★ **DRESSAGE TESTS**

There are several grades of dressage tests. The simplest give you an opportunity to show how well-established your pony's paces are, and how accurately he makes the transition from one to another.

At novice and elementary level, you have to show your pony's obedience by asking him to step backward. In some tests you have to show how balanced and responsive your pony is by lengthening and shortening the steps at walk, trot and canter, or to show that he can step forward and sideways at the same time.

The walk

➤ In dressage, each pace can be executed in various forms including medium, collected, extended and free.

Medium paces are rhythmical and energetic with medium-length strides. In *collected* movements, the horse takes short, elastic steps while in the *extended* version he should reach out and cover as much ground as possible. Finally, *free* paces are on a loose rein, with the horse relaxed but attentive. Start off by practising a medium walk.

∨ Warming up before a competition, when the horse has become tense, tight in the neck and the four-time rhythm has been lost.

The trot

▲ Whether you choose to do a rising or sitting trot – and whatever variation you're practising – your horse should take regular strides forward, changing evenly from one pair of diagonal legs to the other. His energy should come from his hindquarters, propelling him forward.

▼ Trotting with lots of energy is Regina Moldan on Dacapo, riding for Austria in the European Dressage Championships.

The canter

➤ Once you and your pony are moving in harmony at the walk and trot, you can concentrate on the canter. In this three-time movement your pony should bound forward energetically.

Make sure you are sitting upright in the centre of the saddle with your weight evenly distributed. This gives a pony complete freedom of movement.

The hindlegs must produce enough force to give a good rhythmical pace. The leading hindleg should tuck forward under the horse.

The aids

Dressage is the basis for whatever else you want to do with a horse. It teaches you to give, and the horse to receive, a range of subtle instructions and messages.

Communicating

Communication between horse and rider is one of the most important aspects of dressage training. You have to ask the horse to perform any action simply by using signals.

Squeezing with either or both legs, feeling the reins, or pushing with the seat are your only signals when asking the horse to make a huge number of movements. These range from halt and walk to turning and circling – right up to the advanced dressage movements of piaffe and passage.

In dressage your aim is to *perfect* your aids. The means by which you transmit your instructions remain the same, but your interpretation and transmission of them must improve and become more precise.

◄ **This horse** is being warmed up and he has become a little short in the neck with his face coming behind the vertical (see page 18).

Checking the basics

You and your horse are building on the basis of what you have already learnt. So before moving on to anything new, check your position and run through the aids to make sure you haven't slipped into bad habits.

Your seat should be correct: well-balanced, but relaxed. Your body weight must be supported evenly on the two seat bones. As your aids become more subtle, your horse will assume that a momentary stiffening of your back is an instruction and act accordingly. So you must be balanced perfectly and not wriggle about, because it could be misinterpreted.

Riding is done mainly with the legs: they apply most of the aids and create energy in the horse. You must be correctly placed to close the legs inward, encouraging the horse forward.

The stirrup leathers should hang vertically and the *ball* of your feet should sit on the stirrup irons. This is the best position for applying the leg aid. The legs must not wobble around, otherwise the horse may be confused as to whether or not he is receiving an aid. And the upper half of your leg should stay ►

★ **LEFT AND RIGHT REIN**

In dressage riding the horse is said to be on the left or the right rein, even when he is going straight ahead. This is because eventually, at the end of the straight line, he will turn left or right.

So when a 'change of rein' is mentioned, this simply means a change of direction.

Using signals

As you progress with dressage, your aids need to become more precise so that the horse understands exactly what you want him to do. You can also use artificial aids when you practise to back up your natural aids. These sharpen the horse's reaction to your instructions.

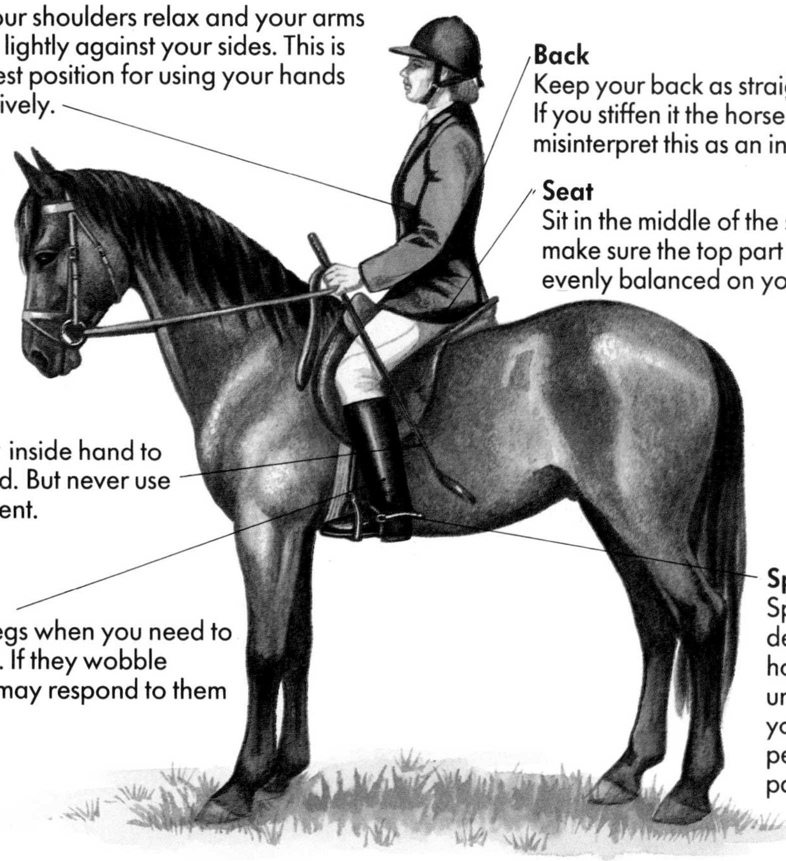

Arms
Let your shoulders relax and your arms brush lightly against your sides. This is the best position for using your hands effectively.

Back
Keep your back as straight as possible. If you stiffen it the horse may misinterpret this as an instruction.

Seat
Sit in the middle of the saddle and make sure the top part of your body is evenly balanced on your seat bones.

Whip
Carry a whip in your inside hand to reinforce your leg aid. But never use the whip as punishment.

Legs
Only move your legs when you need to give an instruction. If they wobble around the horse may respond to them as an aid.

Spurs
Spurs help give a definite leg aid to the horse. Don't use them until you can keep your lower leg perfectly still at any pace.

'BETWEEN LEG AND HAND'

Between the leg and the hand is a term often used in dressage. It means that the horse is alert and ready to respond to any command. Energy has been created by the legs and seat, but is being controlled by the hands. This is the ideal position for horse and rider to be in.

absolutely still at all times in dressage.

Sit upright with your shoulders relaxed and let the top part of your arm fall softly against your body. The inside of your sleeve should brush against the side of your jacket. Your elbow should be soft and supple, allowing the horse to adjust the height of his head and the length of his neck with equal ease.

The voice is a useful aid for practice sessions. When you are training you use it to help the horse understand what you are asking him to do. However, in a dressage test you are not allowed to use your voice and you are penalized if you do. You are being tested on the *unspoken* communication between you and your horse.

Artificial aids

The artificial aids are the whip and the spur. These are used as a back-up for the natural aids. In some junior competitions a whip is not allowed, but you may use spurs.

In dressage training, you can carry a long schooling whip to reinforce the leg aid. Dressage whips are longer and narrower than all-purpose whips. This makes them flexible so that you can lightly flick the horse without taking your hands off the reins.

The whip should not be used as punishment. It helps to sharpen your horse's reaction to your leg aid and reduces the need to kick.

The whip should be carried in the inside hand because the inside leg aids are the most important. They are, therefore, the aids which need to be reinforced. You must remember to change the whip to your other hand when you cross the arena.

Spurs are used when a more definite leg aid is required and more energy from the hindquarters is needed. You should only begin to use spurs when you can maintain an independent leg position. If you can't keep your lower leg still, you may hurt the horse.

The advantage of spurs is their precision: you can apply pressure on an exact spot, while your boot heel gives a rather 'woolly' aid.

➤ **The aim** of a dressage test is to show off the results of all your hard work at home. So a whip is valuable for schooling sessions but need not be used in the ring.

Practising the half halt

The half halt, when a rider asks a horse for a halt but then allows him to go forward, checks a horse's speed at any pace and helps make his strides more springy.

To make a half halt, rest the legs on the horse's sides and restrain the forward movement by giving and taking with the reins. Just as he is about to change the pace ease the reins slightly while keeping the legs firmly on his sides. Asking a horse to slow down and then allowing him to continue helps rebalance him.

Circling

The circle is one of the most basic school movements and it is a good exercise to start practising. It takes some time to make the circle geometrically exact, so don't expect too much from your first attempts. Work on large circles – about 24 metres (26 yards) around – to begin with. The smaller the circle, the more difficult the movement becomes.

To achieve an exact circle, you must give precise instructions. Your horse should be bent slightly round the edge of the circle. On a clockwise circle he should curve a little round your right leg. You ask him to bend to the inside with the fingers of your inside hand, but it is vital to keep a steady contact with your outside hand. Never pull back on the reins.

The touch of your inside leg encourages the horse to go steadily forward, while your outside leg is ready to control the hindquarters if they swing out.

◄ **The circle** is a basic dressage movement that takes some time to perfect. Here the rider has her pony nicely bent to the inside.

▼ **Start your practice circles** with turns on a corner. Concentrate on giving precise signals with your hands and legs to control the horse's movements.

The paces

The well-trained horse can vary his stride in each pace: he takes longer or shorter steps when asked to do so by his rider.

Variations of pace

Variations in the length of step are known as working, collected, medium and extended paces.

Working paces are generally those natural to the horse before he has had much training. He should be obedient, relaxed and balanced, and move with plenty of energy.

Collected paces: The three big joints of the hindlegs – the hip, stifle and hock – are more flexed and the horse's legs tuck well underneath his body at each step. The horse moves with a shorter, rounder action than in the working paces. The croup is lowered, making the forehand light. The neck is raised and arched and the front of the face is almost vertical.

Medium paces: The horse takes steps which are longer than those of a working pace, but not to the fullest possible extent. He must go with great energy, stretching his head and neck forward a little so he can take longer steps with the forelegs as well as the hindlegs.

Extended paces: The horse strides along with maximum energy, taking steps of the greatest possible length.

The walk

The term 'working walk' is not used: because the horse does not have much scope to lengthen or shorten his walk strides, he could not manage four variations of this gait. The horse works most naturally at 'medium walk'; from there the rider can ask him to work at 'free walk on a long rein'.

This means the rider lets the reins out far enough to allow the horse to stretch his head and neck forward and down. He continues to walk with long, deliberate, generous steps.

Giving the aids

To make your pony shorten or lengthen his steps takes lots of practice and patience, and you will certainly need help from your instructor. The first step is to establish good working paces. You can then ask your pony to take a few lengthened steps, making sure he maintains his balance.

This can be done from either working

◄ **This pair are** showing a good working trot. The hindleg is showing good activity and the rider has a good contact in the hands.

★ **TEMPO**

The 'tempo' of the horse's work (the speed of the rhythm) should stay the same in collected, working, medium or extended paces.

When the horse takes medium or extended steps, he is not increasing the number of steps by running. He goes faster because the steps are longer, not quicker.

▲ **Dressage tack:** For the experienced horse and rider, a double bridle helps in giving precise aids. The dressage saddle is specially designed to help the rider sit upright. It has a deep seat to keep you central in the saddle, and a straighter cut because of the longer leg position.

trot or canter. Make a half halt to balance your pony and get his full attention. Then apply both legs to encourage him to take longer, more powerful steps with the hindlegs. At the same time, let him stretch his head and neck forward a little, while keeping the rein contact.

He should lengthen his outline and take longer steps with his forelegs to match those of his hindlegs. He must keep a clear rhythm, taking steps of equal length. Your instructor will be able to tell you if you've succeeded. When your pony does achieve the lengthening you've asked for, make sure you give him plenty of praise.

At the end of the lengthened steps, it is important to make a smooth transition back to the working pace. Sit up, apply both legs and resist slightly with your hands. As soon as he shortens his steps back to the working pace, relax your hands but keep your legs against him and ride forward. Otherwise he will lose his impulsion and slow down.

Impulsion and collection

Impulsion is the power that the horse creates with his hindlegs. It must not be confused with speed. It is controlled energy produced in the horse by the use of your legs and seat. This energy is received in your hands where it is lightly guided and controlled.

You need impulsion to obtain collection. The object of collection is to 'coil up the spring' of energy in the hindquarters. Once the spring is uncoiled, the energy is released and the horse goes into longer steps.

To collect your pony, he must be submissive and not opposing you. The muscles of his neck and jaw should be relaxed. You cannot try to *force* collection by resisting with your hands.

By using your legs, you ask him for more action from the three major joints of the hindlegs. When the pony uses these joints more he steps further underneath himself with his hindlegs. This causes the croup to lower, which in turn raises the forehand. When this happens, you have obtained a degree of collection.

Once the pony is collected you can ask for medium and eventually extended paces. To do this, you maintain or increase the energy with your legs and let the pony go forward from your hands.

The walk

Working paces

Free walk on a long rein

Collected paces

Collected walk

Medium paces

Medium walk

Extended paces

Extended walk

The trot

Working trot

Collected trot

Medium trot

Extended trot

The canter

Working canter

Collected canter

Medium canter

Extended canter

Lateral work

WORK ON BOTH REINS

Most ponies have a 'stiff' side, on which they find certain work more difficult, so they tend to favour their good side as often as they can. You have probably already noticed this in your pony, and certainly will when practising lateral work.

Although it is best to start a new exercise on the rein your pony finds easier, it is important to do every exercise on *both* reins – whether schooling, lungeing or lateral work – to develop suppleness.

As dressage tests become more advanced, the horse is asked to do 'lateral work', or 'work on two tracks' – the hindfeet follow a different track from the forefeet. This happens when he moves sideways, or forward and sideways at the same time, and demonstrates his suppleness, balance and agility.

Turn on the forehand

You have probably asked your horse to go sideways already without noticing it. Think when someone is mucking out a stable with the horse tied up in it. Once they have done one half, they say 'over', and he moves across the stable, making it easier to muck out the other half.

The movement that the horse makes is a sort of 'turn on the forehand', which is one of the first mounted exercises you do when starting lateral work. The turn on the forehand is a useful exercise for three main reasons:

- It teaches your pony to move away from your leg.
- It teaches you to 'blend' the aids given with your legs and your hands.
- It has many everyday uses, such as when opening gates or turning in confined spaces.

In this exercise the pony turns in a half-circle through 180°, so that he changes the direction in which he is facing. It starts from a good, square halt. The outside forefoot marks time (stepping up and down in the same place) and he pivots around it.

The inside forefoot makes a small half-circle around the pivoting outside forefoot, and the hindfeet make a large half-circle to complete the turn.

Giving the aids

The turn on the forehand is made almost entirely with leg aids. The hands do very little. To make a turn to the right (in which you start on the left rein and

Aids for turn on the forehand

1 The start of a turn on the forehand to the left. Make sure the horse is on the bit and listening to you. With your left hand, ask him to look slightly to the left – gently, not pulling, or he may think you want him to step backward.

2 Keep a constant contact on the right rein to prevent the horse stepping forward. Keep your right leg in contact with his side so he doesn't step backward.

end up on the right rein), your pony should first be standing square and on the bit.

Ask him to look slightly to the left by giving little squeezes with the fingers on your left hand, until you can just see his left eye. *Don't pull back* on the reins with this hand, or your pony may be tempted to step backward, which is a serious fault.

Your right hand keeps a steady contact, ready to tell the pony that he is not to step forward.

Apply your left leg just behind the girth, encouraging him to keep up into your hands, and to step sideways.

Your right leg remains in contact with the pony's side, and helps to stop him from stepping backward.

Once the turn is complete, ride the pony energetically forward without hesitation. You must ride forward im-

Turn on the forehand

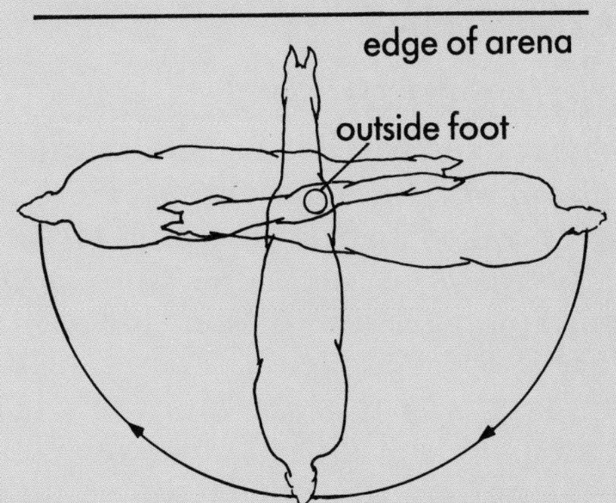

In this exercise the pony turns through 180°. Apart from a slight bending of his head away from the direction in which he is turning, his body remains straight. He pivots around his outside forefoot (shown), the inside forefoot describing a small half-circle and the hindfeet describing a large half-circle.

3 Apply your left leg a little behind the girth, to ask him to turn his hindquarters through the half-circle. Keep your leg on throughout the turn – it should be as fluid as possible, not stopping-and-starting. As soon as you have finished the turn, ride forward straight away. The turn on the forehand is still a *forward* movement, so you don't want him to get the idea that he is going to have a rest when he's finished!

mediately so that the pony maintains his forward impulsion, with his hind legs underneath him.

Yielding to the leg

The next exercise that is usually taught in lateral work is 'leg-yielding'. Here the pony is asked to walk or trot forward and sideways at the same time, while remaining parallel to the side of the arena.

An easy way to start this work is to use an exercise that is known as 'yielding to the leg'. It sounds the same as leg-yielding but is not.

Starting on a 20m (66ft) circle (in walk to begin with, and later in trot), ask your pony to make the circle gradually smaller. You could make it a metre (3ft 3in) smaller on each circuit, down to about 12m (39ft).

Keeping the pony bent on the track of the circle – but not with too much bend

Yielding to the leg

20m (66ft) circle
16m (52ft) circle
1
2
3
4
5
6
7
8

Here you are reducing the size of the circle in stages, from 20m (66ft) down to 12m (39ft).

Yielding to the leg – you ask the pony to step forward and sideways back out to the 20m (66ft) circle.

▼ **Yielding to the leg** on a circle. This is a useful exercise for getting the feel of leg-yielding – where your pony moves forward and sideways at the same time.

in his neck – use your inside leg just at the girth to ask him to step forward and sideways back out to the 20m (66ft) circle.

When doing this in trot, it is best to make sitting trot from about the 16m (52ft) circle downward, and when 'yielding to the leg'. This is because it is difficult to rise to the trot on very small circles and still maintain a rhythmical, balanced trot.

When you reach the 20m (66ft) circle start rising again. The work should be done as evenly as possible on both reins. Your pony will almost certainly find it easier one way than the other.

Leg-yielding

When you can do 'yielding to the leg' fairly easily on both reins, try 'leg-yielding' on a straight line, first in walk and then in trot.

It is best if you can start this work in a 20 × 40m (66 × 132ft) arena, so that you can measure exactly what you are doing. On the left rein, start the exercise by making a half 10-metre (33-foot) circle from M or K to bring you on to the centre line (C to A).

Once your pony is moving straight on the centre line, ask him with your inside leg (the left leg on the left rein) to move sideways as well as forward toward the opposite quarter marker K or M. Try to keep the pony parallel to the side of the arena by keeping your outside leg against him to encourage him forward.

Be content with just two or three steps in 'leg-yielding' to start with, then ride the pony straight forward with both legs. As with any new exercise, praise your pony when he achieves what you are asking him to do.

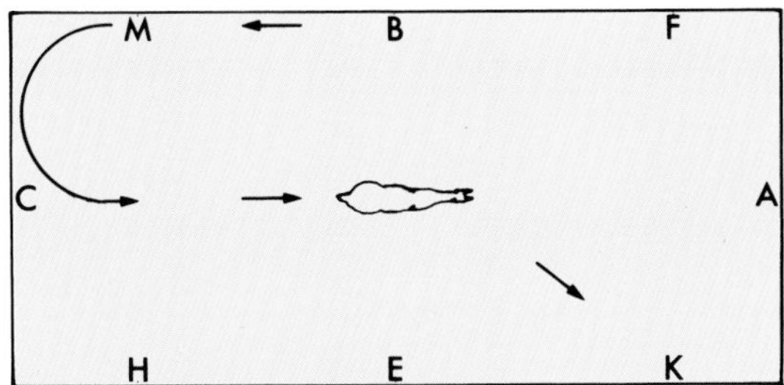

▲ ➤ **Leg-yielding to the right:** Here the horse is stepping forward and sideways with his off-fore/near-hind diagonal pair at trot. The near-hind is in fact following the track made by the off-fore, which does not happen when trotting in a straight line. The pony's body should remain parallel to the side of the arena throughout the exercise.

▲ **Tanya Larrigan and Diplomat** worked at advanced levels in dressage; a horse at this level of competition has to be very obedient and athletic.

When you have mastered the early lateral work exercises of turn on the forehand and leg yielding, you can begin to work toward the movements that are required in the more advanced dressage tests.

Shoulder-in

In correct shoulder-in the horse works with collection. The forehand is taken in from the track and he should be bent throughout his whole length (from poll to tail) around the rider's inside leg.

Introduce your pony to shoulder-in when he can make the turn on the forehand, and leg-yield satisfactorily. Try the exercise in walk to start with, as this gives both you and the pony more time to think about what you are trying to achieve.

The walk should be energetic with impulsion. Increase the degree of collection with half halts so the pony is working on the collected side of medium walk. Down the long side of the arena, put him into a circle of about 8m (26ft) diameter. This establishes the bend needed to perform the exercise correctly.

When the pony rejoins the track at the end of the circle, ask him to take the first step of a second circle. But, as he does this, use your outside hand to check his progress on the circle and your inside leg, applied just by the girth, to encourage him forward along the track. Aim to take the forehand in to an angle of up to about 30°, and keep the hindlegs on the original track.

Your inside hand and leg maintain the bend, while your outside hand keeps him from moving off the track. Your outside leg should be ready to use just behind the girth to stop his hindquarters swinging out.

▼ **Shoulder-in:** The horse is working on the right rein, with his forehand taken in from the track. He is bent around the inside leg of the rider, and is looking *away* from the direction in which he is moving. He is at an angle of up to about 30° to the wall.

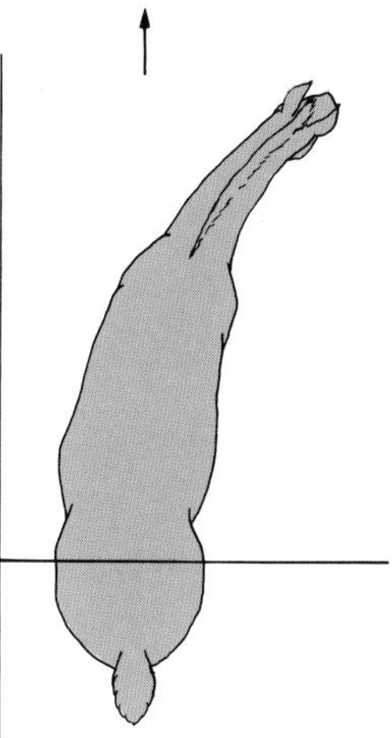

◄ **Shoulder-in** is an excellent schooling exercise as well as a movement required in the dressage test. It improves collection, suppleness, agility, co-ordination and balance.

It helps to straighten a crooked horse in all paces, it can improve the transition to canter and is very effective in preparing the horse to lengthen his strides. It is one of the most useful movements in the training of the dressage horse.

The aids for travers

1 When you are first practising travers – in walk to give yourself time to think – start with an 8m (26ft) circle so you are on the correct bend from the word go.

2 As you come off the circle, when the pony's head is pointing straight down the track, apply your outside leg behind the girth to ask the hindlegs to step sideways.

After three or four steps in shoulder-in, apply both legs and ride the pony forward on the circle on which he is bent. This is an easier way for him to finish the exercise than to be brought back straight on to the track.

Your pony will probably find this exercise easier on one rein than the other. To ensure that you develop him equally on both sides, work as evenly as possible on both reins.

Travers

Travers is a quarter-controlling exercise. The horse's forefeet continue up the track in a straight line, and he looks in the direction in which he is going. The hindquarters are taken in from the track, so that his outside hindleg crosses in front of his inside hindleg.

The best way to introduce your pony to this work is, in walk, to make the 8m (26ft) circle that you made to start the shoulder-in.

At the end of the circle, when his nose and ears are pointing straight down the track, bring your outside leg back and apply the aid just behind the girth. This asks the pony to step sideways with his hindlegs and keep the hindquarters in from the track.

The hindfeet are brought in just enough for him to be making three lines of tracks on the school floor. The outside line is made with the outside forefoot, the middle line with the inside fore and the outside hindfoot, and the inside line with the inside hindfoot.

Ask for just three or four steps in travers – this is enough to begin with – then apply both legs and ride the pony straight up the track.

Travers can eventually be done in trot and canter. Care should be taken in canter, as some horses escape from the correct canter by bringing the hindfeet in from the track and going crookedly.

Renvers

Renvers is the same exercise as travers but the tail is to the wall instead of the head, and the forehand is taken in, on to the inside track. It is a more difficult exercise to achieve, because you don't have the help of the side of the arena to guide the forehand.

3 Your inside leg maintains bend and impulsion, your inside hand lightly varies the rein pressure to keep the flexion, and your outside hand controls the amount of bend.

4 After just three or four steps in travers, bring the pony's hindquarters back on to the track with your inside leg, and ride purposefully forward to maintain impulsion.

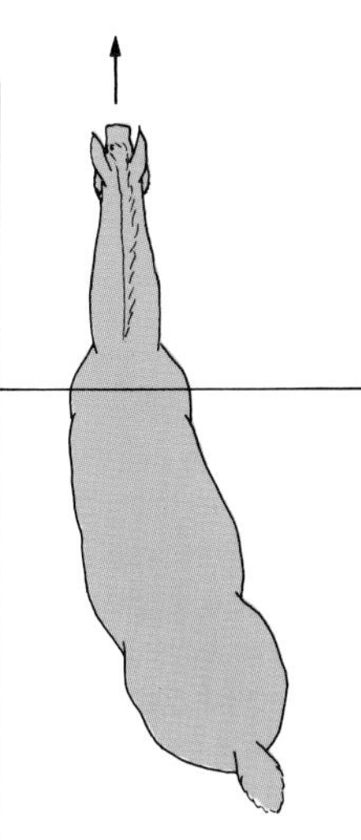

▲ **Travers:** The horse's forefeet continue up the track in a straight line and he looks in the direction in which he is moving. He is slightly bent around the rider's inside leg. His hindquarters are displaced inward from the track so that his hindlegs cross over at each step.

It is best started by making half an 8m (26ft) circle, in walk, coming off the track about three-quarters of the way down the long side. At the end of the half circle – which has established the bend and changed the rein – bring your outside leg back to ask the hindfeet to step sideways.

The fingers of your outside hand ask the forefeet to continue straight down the arena, while your inside hand and leg help to maintain the required bend. The exercise should be made on three lines of tracks, similar to travers.

Start the work on the rein that the pony finds easier and, when some progress has been made, change to the rein that he finds more difficult.

After a short spell on this rein, and certainly before he starts to resist or the work deteriorates in some other way, change back to his easier rein.

Never work for long periods on the side that the pony finds difficult, trying to force him to soften in that direction. Take it slowly and with time he should become more evenly balanced.

Renvers

▲ **Begin with half** a small (8m/26ft) circle to establish the correct bend, at the end of which your outside leg (the right leg above) moves the hindquarters sideways.

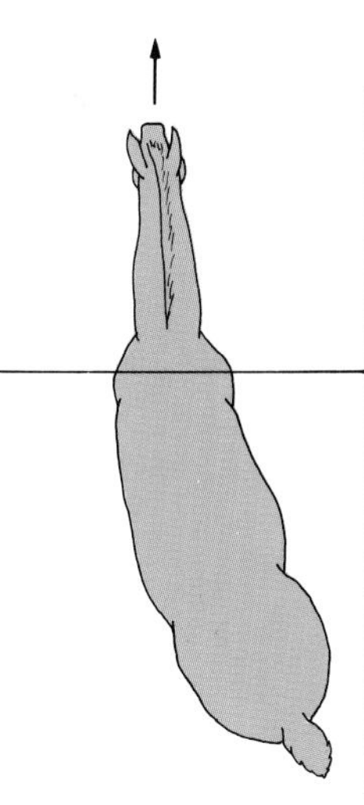

▲ **Renvers:** The same exercise as travers, but here the *forehand* is taken on to the inside track, rather than the hindquarters – the horse is 'tail to the wall' instead of 'head to the wall'. Travers and renvers are good suppling exercises.

Canter exercises

▼ **The 'flying change'** is an exercise where the horse changes the canter lead *during* the canter stride. The horse's obedience, balance and suppleness in canter and canter transitions must be firmly established before this advanced work can be attempted. The 'counter-canter' and the 'simple change of leg' are two important exercises in preparing for the flying change.

One of the most important aims of dressage is to show that the horse's basic paces – walk, trot and canter – are well established. The 'counter-canter' and the 'simple change of leg' are two advanced exercises which demonstrate that the horse is obedient, supple and well-balanced in his canter.

Counter-canter

The canter is a pace in three-time in which the feet come to the ground in the order: outside hind – inside hind and outside fore together – inside fore (or *leading leg* as it is sometimes called). After the inside foreleg comes off the ground there is a moment of suspension when there are no feet on the ground at all. Then the stride starts again with the outside hindleg.

'Counter-canter' simply means that the horse is cantering to the left with the right fore leading, or to the right with the left fore leading. He *must*, however, be under control and well balanced.

Sometimes you see a horse or pony cantering on the 'wrong' leading leg by mistake. He is usually on the forehand, out of balance and going too fast. This shouldn't be confused with correct, intentional counter-canter.

Making a loop

A simple and effective way to introduce counter-canter is to make a shallow loop, about 2m (6ft), off the long side of the arena in canter. As with any new exercise, start your training on the rein that your pony prefers – most horses find canter easier on one rein than the other.

As you go round the short side of the arena, make your canter a little on the collected side of working canter by using

half halts. This ensures that the pony is in good balance to make the shallow loop on the next long side. As you pass the quarter-marker, guide the pony into the loop with your inside hand, holding your inside leg just at the girth to keep him going forward.

Throughout the counter-canter the pony must continue to be bent toward his inside foreleg. So, while you lead him back to the track with the fingers of your outside hand and your inside leg, your inside hand must help to maintain the correct bend.

As in all canter work, your outside leg is positioned ready to control the hindquarters should they tend to swing out. The counter-canter is a very good exercise for testing your ability to blend your leg and hand aids.

Obedience and balance

The shallow loop that you make must be a true loop with the pony's hindfeet following in the line of tracks made by his forefeet. He should not make a sort of 'half-pass' off the track and then 'leg-yield' back on to the track.

When your pony can do this work well on both reins, gradually increase the size of the loop to 4, 5 and 6m (13, 16 and 20ft). Eventually, he can be taken right across the arena from quarter-marker to quarter-marker and ridden in counter-canter through the corner.

The counter-canter should not be ridden for too long – perhaps half a circuit of the arena at most. At the end of the exercise, bring the pony back to trot and after a few steps, ask him to strike off again in true canter. This is to make sure that he remains obedient to the canter aids.

A common mistake is that the pony

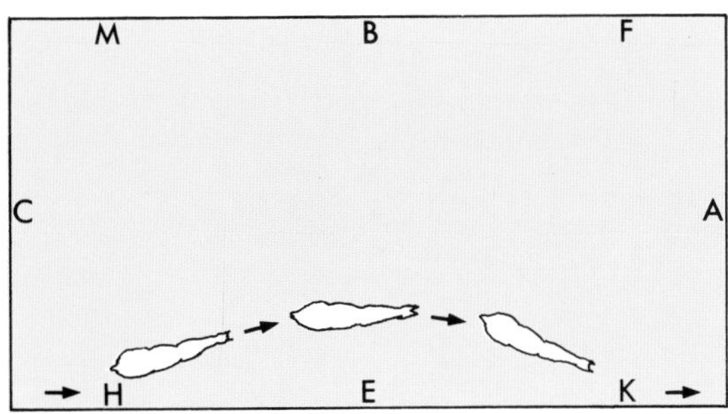

◄ **Counter-canter** training is best begun by making a loop – shallow at first (2m/6ft) and deeper as you progress – off the long side of the arena. Here the horse is cantering on the left rein and is asked to make a loop between H and K. Returning to the track from the loop, he is cantering to the *right*, but his left fore is still the canter lead. The counter-canter is a good suppling exercise.

The counter-canter

1 Establish a canter that is a little on the collected side of working canter, then make a small loop off the long side of the arena. As you pass the quarter-marker, guide the horse into the loop with the fingers of your inside hand, and use your inside leg to maintain forward impulsion.

2 Throughout the loop, the horse should remain on the correct bend – his head and neck should be slightly flexed toward the leading leg. You may need to carry your outside leg just behind the girth, as in the aid for canter, to help his co-ordination.

3 Lead the horse back to the track with the fingers of your outside hand and your inside leg. Use your inside hand to maintain the correct bend, and have your outside leg ready to prevent the hindquarters from swinging out – the hindfeet must follow in the line of tracks made by the forefeet.

Early training for simple change

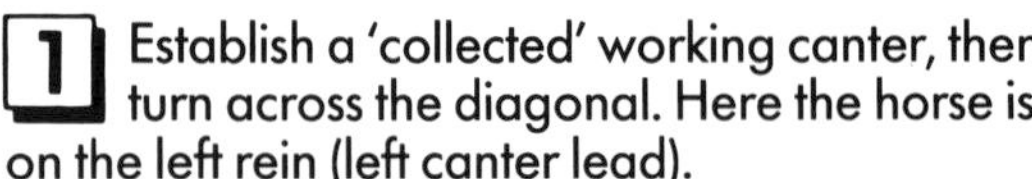

1 Establish a 'collected' working canter, then turn across the diagonal. Here the horse is on the left rein (left canter lead).

2 As you approach 'X' (the centre), make the downward transition to rising trot. Half halt to balance, then go into sitting trot as you approach the next quarter-marker, and change the bend to the right.

★ **ON THE FOREHAND**
A horse is said to be 'on the forehand' when too much of his weight is on his front end. More of the weight should be carried by his hindquarters, with the forehand acting as a 'support'. A pony that is on the forehand is not using himself correctly because the hindlegs, instead of being underneath him, are trailing behind. The problem is worse at faster gaits, where he is doing little more than 'running' along out of balance. It is often (but not always) combined with a low head carriage, and he feels 'heavy' in the rider's hands. A horse with this problem must be encouraged to flex the joints of his hindlegs more, so the croup lowers and the forehand lightens.

'falls' out of counter-canter due to loss of balance or co-ordination. To help avoid this, take care to maintain the correct bend, and keep your outside leg back as the canter aid to remind the pony which leg he is supposed to be on.

Remember here that the outside leg is the one on the outside of the bend of the pony, and *not* necessarily the outside of the arena.

Simple change

The simple change of leg at canter is an exercise where the horse changes the canter lead through two or three steps in walk. It is an important exercise in confirming his obedience to the canter aids, and it improves his balance.

While the more advanced dressage rules require that the simple change be made through the walk, the more elementary tests allow it to be made through trot and walk. Certainly, in his early training you should introduce the exercise to your pony progressively: canter – trot – walk – trot – canter.

When you are sure that your pony will strike off in canter to the left and right, accurately and without resistance, you can go on to teaching him the simple change.

It is best started, once again, from a canter a little on the collected side of his working canter. When you have achieved this, by the use of half halts, turn across the diagonal from 'M' to 'K', and trot as you approach 'X'. Half halt once again to ensure a well-balanced trot by the time you reach 'K'.

As you approach 'K' go into sitting trot and change the bend to the left. This should create the ideal conditions to ask the pony to canter left in the corner between 'K' and 'A'. This completes your first attempt at the simple change.

Direct transitions

When you can do this equally well on both reins, the next stage is to ask the pony to trot as you approach 'X' on the diagonal, go into sitting trot, change the bend and ask him to canter at the next quarter-marker. As his training progresses, reduce the number of trot steps between the two canters down to about three.

During this time it is very useful to work on the canter to walk and walk to canter transitions, called *direct transitions*, but don't include them in the simple change at this stage.

As your simple change through trot and your direct transitions improve, you can start to make the simple change: canter – trot – walk – trot – canter. Then gradually reduce the number of steps in trot until you achieve the proper simple change: canter – walk – canter.

3 At first, ask your pony for the new (right leg) canter lead in the corner between the quarter-marker and A or C. Next you can ask for the canter at the quarter-marker itself, and eventually reduce the number of steps in trot down to three.

! AVOID BOREDOM
Take your time when introducing any new work to your pony. Problems are often created by trainers who rush their work and ask their horses to go on to the next stage before they are ready. If your pony makes his first simple change well, reward him and change the subject. It is a mistake to be too greedy and to continue on one subject for too long – boredom often creates resistance.

The simple change

▲ **The true simple change** is the sequence canter – walk – canter. This requires you to make *direct transitions,* which means you go from canter to walk then walk to canter with no steps of trot in between. Work on these *before* including them in your simple change.

Dressage tests

When you and your pony can perform basic school movements in all paces, you are ready to take a dressage test. The 'Preliminary' dressage test is the most basic. Preliminary tests are numbered from one to ten, starting with the easiest and becoming more difficult as you progress.

Elegance and style

Dressage tests the training of the pony, so it is him – not you – that the judge concentrates on. Only ten marks are given to the rider out of a total of 180. The judge takes into consideration the obedience of the pony, and also the freedom of his paces and elegance of his carriage. So if two ponies have the same training, the one that has better natural paces often scores higher.

The object of riding a dressage test at Preliminary level is to show the judge how well your pony can walk, trot and canter. You have a chance to tell her that your pony is well balanced in all his paces. Show her that the pony stays straight on the sides of the arena and bends softly through the corners. Demonstrate the pony's steady 'tempo' in all this work.

The test sheet

The 'test sheet' tells you all the movements you are required to do. It also explains exactly *where* and *when* you do the movements. Make sure you have a copy of the test sheet well before the date of the competition so that you can be familiar with it on the day.

You are allowed to have a 'Commander' – someone who reads the test out for you as you go along. However, it is better to learn it and do it on your own.

Learning the movements

Learning a test by heart makes riding it fluently easier. One way to learn is to mark out the dressage arena in a corner

▼ **In a dressage test,** the horse and rider should be perfectly in tune with each other. Every movement is executed at a specific marker and marks are awarded for accuracy.

of a field. Jog round on foot, making the 'transitions' at the appropriate marker. You can do this at any time – the more often the better!

Practise it on your pony as well, but remember that riding through the complete test too often causes problems. Ponies have very good memories and soon learn the test. They may then anticipate a movement – particularly a transition – and start to do it too early. This is a fault and loses you marks. A safer bet is to practise the movements separately and only put them together as a complete test once or twice a week.

Dressage rules

There are always rules about dress and equipment. The horse is not allowed to wear a martingale, boots or bandages. You must use a plain snaffle bit in a Preliminary test. You should wear a hard hat conforming to safety standards, shirt, collar and tie, fawn, beige or white breeches or jodhpurs, black or brown boots, a tweed jacket and light-coloured gloves. Spurs may be worn and you can carry a whip. However these rules vary for different disciplines, so it is important to read the rules for *each* test carefully before you enter.

Reading the dressage rules thoroughly gives you a fair chance to do well because the judge marks your pony in accordance with them. As you do your test, she asks herself the following:

- Is this pony going energetically forward in all his paces?
- Are his basic paces correct and does he walk, trot and canter in a steady tempo all round the arena, or does he lose his rhythm on turns and circles?
- Does he bend a little to the left throughout his body on the left rein and to the right on the right rein?
- Is he submissive – that is, free from resistance?
- Is he on the bit? ➤

★ REMEMBER YOUR MARKERS

There are several methods of remembering the dressage markers. Try this one:

- ☐ As you enter at 'A', you face the judge at 'C'.
- ☐ 'F', 'B' and 'M' are down the right-hand side – so think of 'Four Big Men'.
- ☐ 'K', 'E' and 'H' are down the left-hand side – think of 'King Edward's House'.

➤ **Encourage your pony** to bend around turns and circles by using your inside leg on the girth and your outside leg behind the girth. Use the inside rein to turn his head slightly in the direction he's bending, and use the outside rein to balance him.

▼ **Collected trot** must have lots of impulsion. Use your legs to push the pony up to the bit and keep the pace steady by giving and taking gently with the reins.

▼ **Most tests require you** to do some movements in sitting trot. To develop a secure seat, plenty of work without stirrups is essential.

● Does this rider apply all of the aids effectively?

The judge gives a mark from 0-10 for each movement, allotted as follows:

10 Excellent
9 Very good
8 Good
7 Fairly good
6 Satisfactory
5 Sufficient
4 Insufficient
3 Fairly bad
2 Very bad
1 Not executed

So, scores of five or six are acceptable to start with, seven or above means that you are doing well. A score of four means that the pony is doing some of the work poorly, perhaps he has the wrong bend, is 'above the bit', 'overbent' or not really going forward.

When the judge gives a mark of four or less she often writes a comment on the score sheet to tell you why she has marked you down. She may also comment on your work when you score five or more. These comments are meant to help you with the training of your pony and to encourage you to do better.

Memory jogger

A helpful way to learn a test is to draw a series of dressage arenas on cards or sheets of paper. Draw in each movement, one in each arena, using a different colour for walk, trot and canter. A change of colour means a transition. Make notes on the arenas to remind you what rein you should be on.

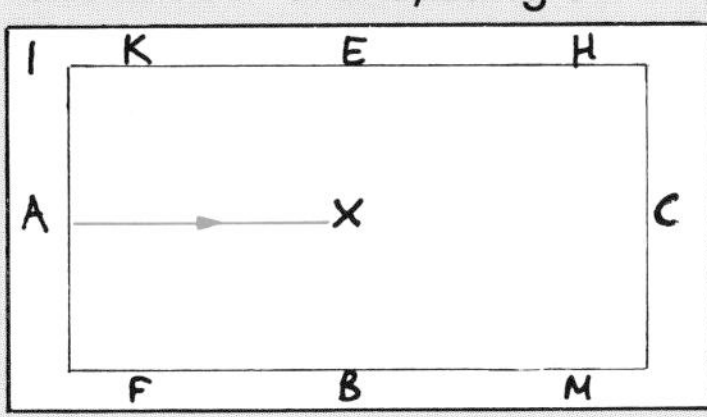

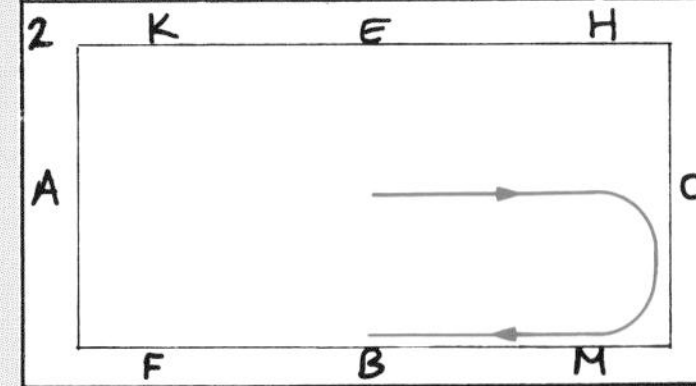

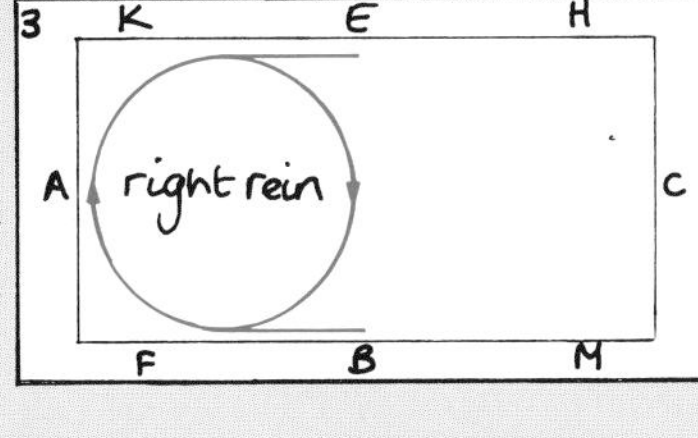

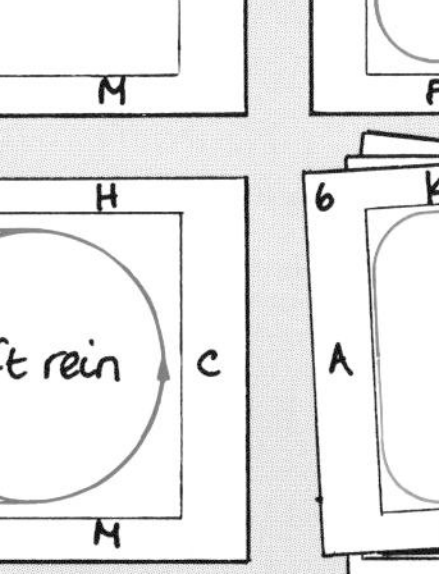

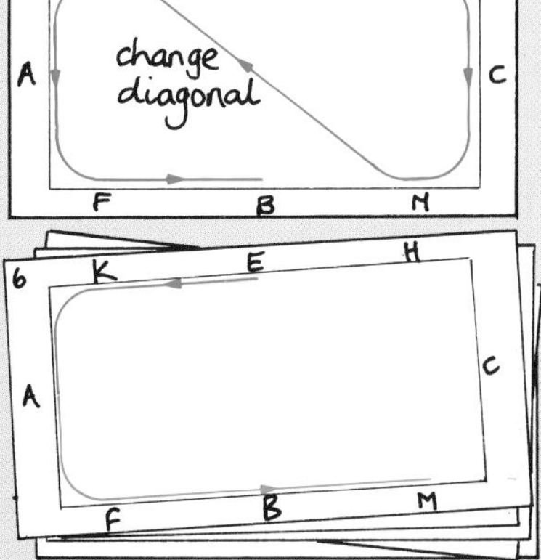

walk — trot — canter —

◄ **The pony** should show no signs of resistance such as tossing his head or flicking his tail. Try to keep his outline the same while going from one pace to another. When making the transition from trot to canter, do a sitting trot and use your legs and seat to push the pony into canter. He should not just quicken his trot!

Dressage test: on the day

▼ **Ride your test** in a fluent way keeping your pony's stride even. When you make transitions, concentrate on keeping them smooth – the pony should not show any signs of resistance such as suddenly raising his head. Remember that accuracy earns points in a dressage test so try to perform each movement at the marker required.

Riding a dressage test is a challenge for you and your pony. Knowing the test thoroughly and practising it at home helps you to perform it with confidence. Follow these guidelines for riding the sample British Dressage (BD) Preliminary test below.

First impressions

The collecting ring steward tells you when it's your turn to compete. Ride quietly around the *outside* of the arena until the judge gives you the signal to start. This is usually a car horn.

A typical British Dressage Preliminary test might start with the instructions: *Enter at working trot at 'A', at 'X' halt and salute, proceed at working trot and at 'C' track left.*

Make sure that you give yourself plenty of room to enter straight at 'A' – this makes it easy for you to ride directly down the centre line. Ask your pony to halt by supporting him with your legs, sitting softly in the saddle and squeezing your fingers on the reins.

Take the reins and whip in your left hand. Lower your right hand to your side and bow from the neck. Ride forward in working trot and rise after about two steps. Turn left at 'C' giving your pony a clear aid in advance.

The test might continue: *From 'H' working trot around the arena to 'F'.* Ride at rising trot in a steady tempo. Ask your pony to bend around each corner using your inside leg. Prepare him for the turn with half halts.

'F' 'X' 'H' change the rein in working trot. As you come out of the 'A'–'F' corner keep the pony bent to the left and ride straight across the diagonal. As you cross 'X' change your diagonal. Ask your pony to bend to the right before you

arrive at the track – this means that he is balanced for the next corner.

'H' working trot around the arena to 'A'. Keep your trot steady and your pony's tempo even. Ask your pony to flex to the inside around the corners.

Canter work

At 'A' commence a 20m circle right, canter between 'X' and 'A'. As you pass 'A', go into sitting trot and start your 20m circle to the right. As you pass 'X', increase your impulsion with your inside (right) leg, sit deep in the saddle and ask your pony to canter.

'A' working canter around the arena, between 'B' and 'F' working trot to 'K'. Keep the pony between your legs and your hands in canter around the arena to 'B'. As you approach 'B', use a half halt to balance him before making the transition from canter to trot between 'B' and 'F'. When you have trotted a few paces, start rising and continue in rising trot until 'K'. Ride the corners carefully.

Change of direction

'K' medium walk, 'E' turn right, 'B' track left, at 'M' working trot. As you approach 'K', use half halts to prepare your pony for the transition to walk. Ride him energetically forward in walk counting the regular four-time beat.

Just before 'E', start your turn and walk across the arena to 'B'. Before you arrive at 'B' ask your pony to bend to the left so that he is ready to turn left at 'B'.

▲ **Most dressage competitions** have more than one arena with different tests going on at the same time. Try not to let this disturb you. Just concentrate on keeping your pony and yourself calm and riding a good test.

BD Preliminary dressage test

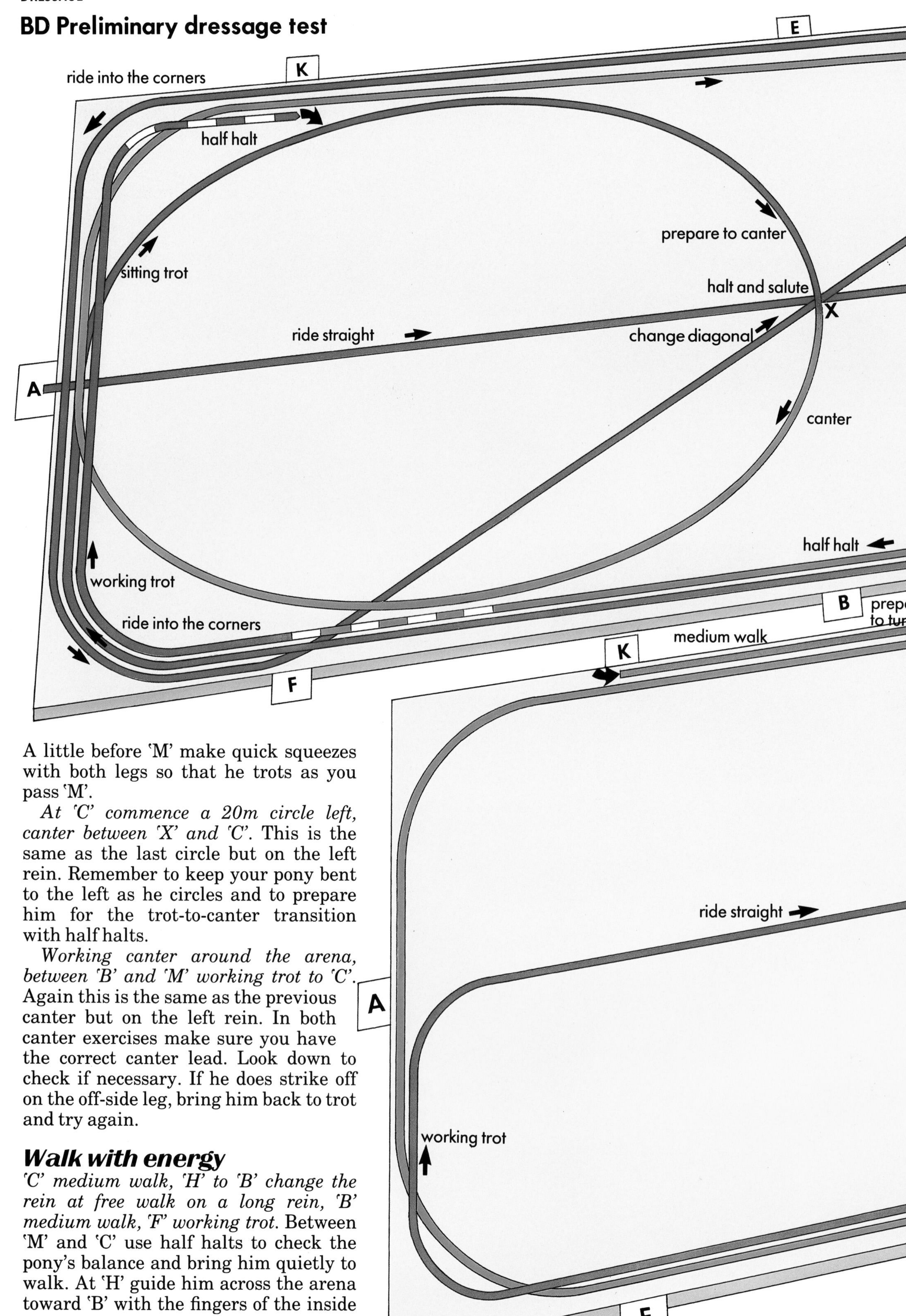

A little before 'M' make quick squeezes with both legs so that he trots as you pass 'M'.

At 'C' commence a 20m circle left, canter between 'X' and 'C'. This is the same as the last circle but on the left rein. Remember to keep your pony bent to the left as he circles and to prepare him for the trot-to-canter transition with half halts.

Working canter around the arena, between 'B' and 'M' working trot to 'C'. Again this is the same as the previous canter but on the left rein. In both canter exercises make sure you have the correct canter lead. Look down to check if necessary. If he does strike off on the off-side leg, bring him back to trot and try again.

Walk with energy

'C' medium walk, 'H' to 'B' change the rein at free walk on a long rein, 'B' medium walk, 'F' working trot. Between 'M' and 'C' use half halts to check the pony's balance and bring him quietly to walk. At 'H' guide him across the arena toward 'B' with the fingers of the inside

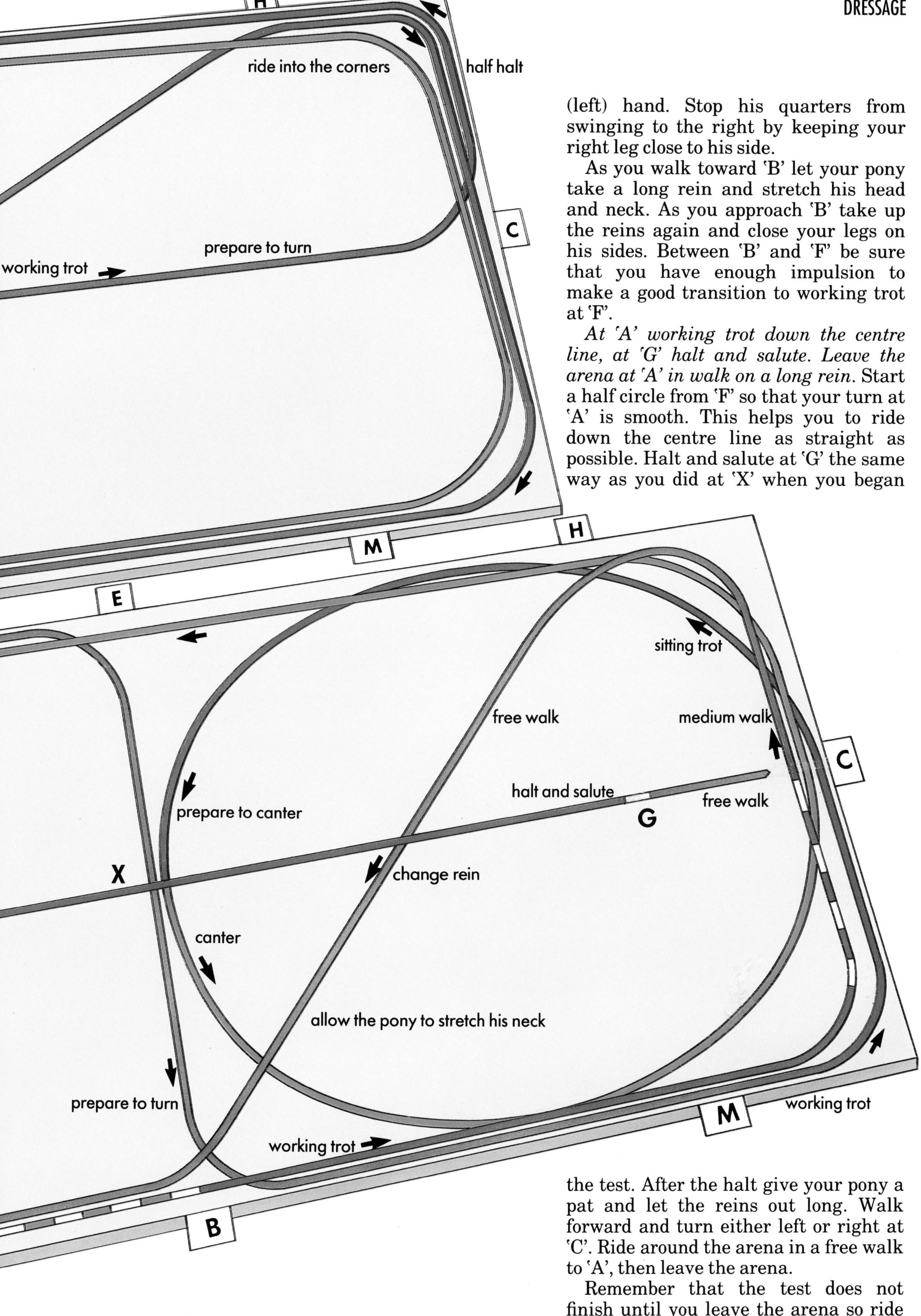

(left) hand. Stop his quarters from swinging to the right by keeping your right leg close to his side.

As you walk toward 'B' let your pony take a long rein and stretch his head and neck. As you approach 'B' take up the reins again and close your legs on his sides. Between 'B' and 'F' be sure that you have enough impulsion to make a good transition to working trot at 'F'.

At 'A' working trot down the centre line, at 'G' halt and salute. Leave the arena at 'A' in walk on a long rein. Start a half circle from 'F' so that your turn at 'A' is smooth. This helps you to ride down the centre line as straight as possible. Halt and salute at 'G' the same way as you did at 'X' when you began the test. After the halt give your pony a pat and let the reins out long. Walk forward and turn either left or right at 'C'. Ride around the arena in a free walk to 'A', then leave the arena.

Remember that the test does not finish until you leave the arena so ride the last free walk carefully.

Dressage test: improvements

There are several tips that can help improve your dressage test results. Accurate school movements score high points, so it's worth spending time practising them at home. Giving your pony a proper warm up also makes a difference to his overall performance.

School movements

Every dressage test requires you to perform some school movements. If your pony performs these well, he is likely to score highly even if he makes some minor mistakes elsewhere in the test.

Circles are the most common school movements included in dressage tests. In a good circle the pony is slightly bent throughout his whole length. He is also tracking up, his hindfeet stepping into or in front of the prints that his front feet have just made.

At novice level, most tests require you to perform a 20m circle. This is half the normal arena. To work out how to ride a circle, draw an arena on a piece of paper and divide it into two by tracing a line between 'B' and 'E'. Then mark four points in one half of it: one at 'A' or 'C', one at 'X' and one at each side of the arena. Draw a line to each point so that you have a square and then draw a circle joining the points together (see above).

Drawing a 20m circle

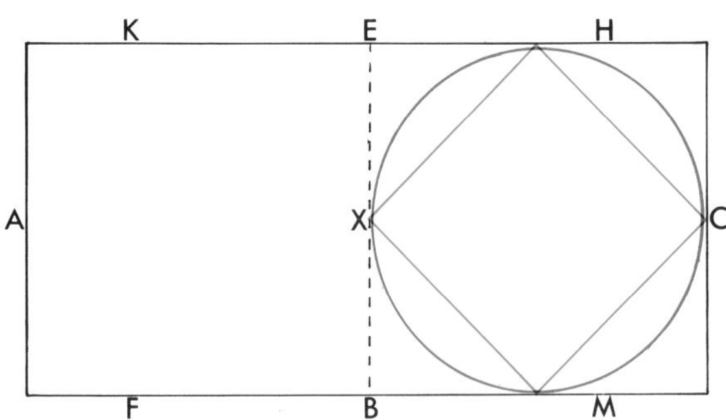

Home schooling

In practice, use cones to mark the four points on the circle and ride toward each point. If you ride quarter circles at ➤

▼ **When performing** school movements such as circles and serpentines, your horse should bend slightly throughout his whole body, not just his head and neck!

Work out your bend carefully beforehand. Ride your horse forward with plenty of energy. Your inside leg creates the impulsion, and your outside leg controls the horse's quarters. Ask him to bend with your inside hand and leg and control the pace with your outside hand. By using each leg and hand independently, you learn to become an effective rider.

➤ **This horse** is going forwards and sideways in a well-controlled half pass so the rider will find it easy to be accurate.

►**Always give yourself** a couple of minutes to make minor adjustments to your tack. A helping hand from a friend is always welcome and it gives you a chance to polish your boots!

▼**Warming up is vital** if you want your pony to perform well in any competition. Some ponies go well if they are lunged for a while before being ridden. Lungeing settles excitable ponies and warms them up at the same time.

each corner you can maintain a curve around the circle.

Most horses are stiffer on one side than the other, so remember to work on your pony's weak side as much as on his good side. He finds it difficult to bend to the inside when you ride a circle on his stiff side, which makes more work for you.

If your pony cannot bend to the inside, try not to let him bend to the *outside*. By allowing your pony to bend to the outside, you are showing the judge that he is stiff – this loses you marks. It's better to perform a circle straight than to bend the wrong way!

Transitions

When you go from one gait to another, your transitions should be as smooth as possible. A rough transition shows that you haven't prepared your pony properly. Always think ahead and warn the pony with half halts if you are changing pace. Practise transitions frequently during your schooling sessions to teach your pony to be responsive.

When the test asks you to change pace at a marker, your pony should begin the new pace as your upper body passes the marker. Changing pace *exactly* at the required marker scores points.

Warming up

On the day of the competition, *always* give yourself plenty of time to arrive well before your test is due to begin. You need to collect your number and see if the tests are running on time.

How much warming up you do depends on your pony. Some ponies need more riding in than others. Some just need to be given a quick canter to wake them up before the test.

Find out how much warm-up time your

pony needs. He should be settled enough to be obedient, but not so tired that he loses his sparkle. Don't try to do any last minute schooling – you'll just make yourself nervous and tense up your pony.

The timing of your warm up is important. When you feel the pony is responsive and supple, stop working and walk him around to keep him relaxed. Don't warm up too early so that you and your pony have to stand about for a long time before the class. On the other hand, make sure that you have a couple of minutes to give a final polish to your boots and your pony before you enter the arena.

If your pony is highly strung and nervous you may find that lungeing him settles him down. Work him evenly on both reins but do not wear him out by too much work: 15-20 minutes is quite long enough to settle and warm him up.

The score sheet

At the end of the competition, when the prizes have been presented and the results announced, you can collect your score sheet from the secretary's office. This is a list of all the movements in the test and shows what marks you received for each movement.

The judge may make a short comment beside some of the movements. These comments are intended to help you, so don't be disheartened if they are a little critical! Read them carefully to see where you did well and where you can make improvements for next time. File them for future reference.

▼ **The time you spend** warming up varies from pony to pony. Some need to be given a canter to get them going, while others perform better if they are ridden in gently. All ponies, however, should be ridden for a short time before they enter the arena, to prepare them for the competition.

4: Eventing

The challenge of eventing

Eventing is a competitive sport made up of three phases: dressage, show jumping and cross country. It is designed to test the discipline, courage and stamina of both horse and rider.

One-day events

A one-day event begins with fairly simple dressage tests which put competitors through a series of basic set movements. These must be performed from memory and should demonstrate the horse's obedience and athleticism at, say, the medium walk, working trot and canter and at a square halt.

Once the dressage phase is completed, all competitors move on to the show-jumping phase. Again, the course is not too demanding: horse and rider must try to complete a clear round by concentrating on accuracy rather than speed.

Finally, riders go on to the cross-country section which, even at novice level, requires determination and bravery. Both horse and rider must be bold and agile enough to jump solid fences, ditches and water jumps arranged along a course which is deliberately challenging and which requires much greater fitness than normal hacking.

Three-day events

In a three-day event, the phases are spread out over three days. The first day is devoted to dressage, the second to

▲ **When riding through water** keep to a steady speed. Your pony may lose his footing if you go too fast. It is also quite hard work for him.

◄ **Cross country** is probably the most exciting section of eventing. You have to tackle a wide variety of obstacles – not only fences but also hills, water jumps and uneven ground.

speed and endurance (which replaces the cross-country stage in a one-day event) and the third day is for show jumping.

The dressage test in a three-day event is more demanding than in a one-day and includes more advanced movements such as the extended walk, trot and canter.

On the second day, the competitors take part in four different phases (A,B,C and D) which make up the speed and endurance test. These phases give both horse and rider a much more gruelling time than the one-day cross-country event and include a roads and tracks test, a steeplechase, a longer roads and tracks test and a cross-country course.

Road and tracks (1): Phase A is a timed hack which is usually organized through woods and round the edge of fields.

A course, which is about 6-7km (3½-4½ miles) long, is marked out. To complete the course within the allowed time, a rider must cover about 1km (5/8th of a mile) in four minutes. To do this, horses maintain a fast trot, with short bursts of cantering and walking in between.

Competitors who do not complete in the given time receive time faults, but there are no extra marks for finishing early!

The steeplechase: Phase B takes place either on a race course or round a large

▲**At novice level** the dressage test includes a medium walk, working trot and canter. Always learn the sequence of movements thoroughly – you often have to perform them from memory.

What to wear

☐ **Hacking jackets,** with a plain stock or tie are essential for Pony Club and British Horse Trials Association (BHTA) novice events. A dark blue or black jacket with a white stock is required for intermediate and advanced competitions.

☐ **Jodhpur boots** are fine but long boots are better for both the dressage and jumping phases because they give more support.

☐ **Gloves** are required for the dressage phase and offer more grip on the reins. It is also advisable to wear gloves with a good grip for the cross-country section.

☐ **Jodhpurs or breeches** can be fawn, buff, yellow or white. Checked, denim or other coloured jodhpurs are not acceptable for eventing.

☐ **Hats** must be worn for all phases of eventing. The Pony Club insists on one of the three following hats: PAS 015, ENI 384 with BSI Kite Mark or SEI, or ASTMF 1163 with BSI Kite Mark or SEI.

☐ **Back or body protectors,** which can be strapped on under your shirt, are advisable. Your back is vulnerable on a horse especially when galloping and jumping during the speed and endurance sections.

TWO-DAY EVENTS

Two-day events are the ideal stepping stone from a one-day to a three-day event. The phases are the same as for a three-day event, but the speed and endurance section is shorter and less demanding.

The first day is taken up by the dressage and show jumping and the second day by a speed and endurance test.

field. It is about 3km (2 miles) long and has between six and ten jumps. Most horses compete at a gallop. Again, a specific time is given to complete the course. At novice level you need to cover 1km (5/8th of a mile) in about $2^1/_2$ minutes.

Roads and tracks (2): Phase C is similar to phase A, but the course is longer.

Ten-minute halt: At this stage in the competition everyone is given time to catch their breath. Riders can plan their tactics for the final, cross-country phase and can make sure that both horse and tack are ready.

The cross-country section: Phase D of a three-day event is taken up with a challenging cross-country course. The course is timed and penalties are incurred for refusals, falls at fences and for not completing in the allowed time.

The cross-country course is $4^1/_2$-$7^1/_2$km ($2^1/_2$- $4^1/_2$ miles) long. The time allowed is based on covering roughly 550m (600yd) per minute.

At the end of the cross-country phase, riders should take special care of their horses and make sure that they are dry, watered, fed and generally comfortable.

The final day

At the beginning of the third day, there is a veterinary inspection of all the horses still competing. The vet makes sure that they are fit enough to go on to the show-jumping section of the event.

The show-jumping course is designed to test whether the horse is still fit and supple enough to jump after the events of the previous two days. The jumping order begins with the lowest-placed competitors and finishes with the leaders – making it an exciting climax to the whole event.

Keys to success

Hard work and patience can pay dividends in improving dressage and show-jumping skills but one of the most important qualities for an event rider is courage. You must be brave and determined enough to compete in the cross-country section as well as have the necessary endurance and fitness that it demands.

Event horses must be willing and obedient. They must also be bold and fearless – and have great trust in their riders.

◄ **Regal Realm** being trotted up for his veterinary inspection after the cross-country stage of a three-day event. Horses must be judged fit enough to go on to the show-jumping section of the competition.

▼ **Ride carefully** as you go round the show-jumping course. You get five penalty points if you knock down an obstacle so a clear round is more important than speed.

Karen Dixon and Get Smart on phase A at Badminton Horse Trials. The three-day event is the ultimate test of horse and rider, and the speed and endurance phases require fitness, concentration and ability from both partners.

Speed and endurance

In two and three-day events the speed and endurance test consists of four separate phases. Phases A and C are 'roads and tracks', B is a steeplechase and D is the cross country. The object of phases A, B and C is to test the horse's all-round fitness, and his ability to cope with phase D – after only a 10-minute break.

Roads and tracks

The purpose of phase A, the first of the two roads and tracks phases, is to warm up the horse before phase B (the steeplechase). It is always shorter than phase C. Phase C acts as a 'winding down period' for the horse after the steeplechase, but it also tests the horse's stamina and ability to recover in time for the cross country.

The length of the roads and tracks varies depending upon the standard, ranging from a total length (A and C combined) of 8-10km (4.9-6.2 miles) for a Junior or Novice event, to 10-13.7km (6.2-8.5 miles) for an Intermediate or Advanced three-day event.

The terrain may vary from roads, to fields or tracks, with all sorts of going to negotiate.

You have to ride phases A and C at a speed of 220m (240yd) per minute, which requires a fairly brisk trot if you are to avoid penalties. You are penalized one point for each second in excess of the optimum (expected) time up to a time limit, after which you are eliminated.

The steeplechase

The steeplechase course may be a variety of designs, but most courses are two circuits over about eight fences in total. The fences are made of sloping birch with a guard rail to help the horse to judge his take-off point. They are no higher than 1.3m (4ft 3in), and at least one has an open ditch.

The speed you ride the course (galloping pace) is 640m (700yd) per minute for Juniors; 650m (710yd) per minute for Novices; and 690m (750yd) per minute for Intermediate and Advanced horses. The length of course ranges from 2-2.7km (1.2-1.7 miles) from Junior through to Advanced.

You are penalized 0.8 of a penalty point for each second you take over the optimum time. Again, there is a time limit, above which you are eliminated.

'Walking' the course

Every two and three-day event holds a 'briefing', when competitors are given a map of the four phases. Technical points are discussed, and you can ask any questions you may have.

After the briefing you go on an organized drive round the roads and tracks. The chief steward or organizer leads the convoy, and points out the red and white turning flags (failing to ride between these means elimination) and the

FITNESS PROGRAMME

The three-day event is a testing and arduous competition, and it is vital that both horse and rider are 100% fit. A fitness programme should be planned for the horse – preliminary roadwork followed by a gradual build-up of work. Some speed work is required, but *too* much puts unnecessary strain on the horse; slow cantering is best as this builds up fitness and stamina without stress or strain.

Hillwork at all paces is one of the best methods of getting a horse fit.

The rider must also be very fit. Running and swimming are helpful exercises to ensure this.

◄ **The steeplechase** is the second phase of speed and endurance, sandwiched between the two 'roads and tracks'. Soaring over these eight or so fences at speed is just one of the tasks required of the bold and versatile event horse.

➤ **How much** an individual horse has to be pushed on the steeplechase depends on his natural speed. This is where your skill as the rider comes into play, knowing how much 'petrol is left in the tank' – bearing in mind that the cross country is yet to come. It may be better to have a couple of time faults on the steeplechase than to push the horse to his absolute limit, particularly if the going is deep.

orange direction markers which tell you where to go. Each kilometre is marked, so make a note of this as well.

The drive includes a stop at the steeplechase so you can walk the course. Study the tightness of the turns, the state of the going, the siting of the fences and the halfway point.

It is a good idea either to drive a second time or to ride your horse round the roads and tracks at a later date (this is permitted). Make a note on your map of the type of going so you know whether to use studs, and where to change pace.

Setting the pace

You don't need to warm your horse up actively before the start of phase A, though it is a good idea to have him walked in-hand for 15-20 minutes to loosen him up. When it is time for you to go you are counted down. Start your stopwatch and check that it is running before the starter says 'Go!'.

Some people prefer to walk and canter on the roads and tracks, while others proceed at a steady trot. Which you choose depends on the type and character of your horse and at what pace he covers the ground most easily.

▼ **Phases A, B and C** follow straight on one after the other, and share the same start/finish enclosure by the steeplechase course.

At a suitable place on phase A, it is important to give the horse a 'pipe-opener' (quick sprint) for a hundred metres or so. This opens his lungs in readiness for the steeplechase.

Stop your stopwatch at the end of phase A, and restart it on your count down for phase B. On the steeplechase establish the necessary speed as quickly as possible, then try to maintain it to avoid time penalties.

There is no advantage in being faster than the optimum time – this only uses up more of the horse's energy than necessary. Check your stopwatch at the halfway point and aim to finish with no more than 15-20 seconds to spare. Don't pull the horse up abruptly – let him slow down gradually.

Veterinary inspection

The second set of roads and tracks is more difficult than the first. Your horse may be reluctant to keep up the pace, so try to make it as easy as possible for him by finding the best ground and sitting lightly on his back.

Allot double time for the first kilometre of phase C, and walk. This gives the horse a chance to recover from the steeplechase. Some riders even dismount and lead their horses for the first kilometre or so. There are no hard and fast rules, you have to judge the best course of action on the day.

At the end of phase C you have to trot your horse through the finish to allow the panel of veterinary surgeons to check that he is sound. They also check his breathing and heart rate. Any horse they consider unfit is not allowed to continue the competition. After phase C there is a compulsory 10-minute 'halt' before the cross country.

▲ **A competitor** checks her stopwatch as she passes a kilometre marker on phase C, the second set of roads and tracks. Most competitors make out a chart on a piece of plastic-covered card so they can check their times at each stage, particularly those on the roads and tracks.

The 'box'

During the 10-minute 'halt' between phases C (the steeplechase) and D (the cross country), horse and rider go into the 'box' – an enclosure at the start of the cross-country course – to prepare.

Here the horse is quickly washed down, his shoes and studs are checked (perhaps with a rapid change of studs for the cross country) and his mouth is rinsed out. His girths and noseband are loosened and he is walked around until his turn to go. Grease is usually applied to the front of his legs in case he hits a fence – this has to be done carefully to avoid getting any on the reins! There is always a vet and a farrier on hand in the 'box'.

Generally, it is the helpers who do most of this work. The rider should try to relax during this time, have something refreshing to drink, and mentally prepare for the cross country ahead.

The day before the speed and endurance phase, an emergency kit of spare tack, veterinary equipment, shoe studs and grooming and washing items (water is provided) should be put together ready for the helpers to take to the 'box', and also to the steeplechase course, where similar checks can be carried out.

Cross country

The thrill of riding and jumping in the open makes cross country the most exciting section of eventing. But you need to be familiar with the jumps – knowing what to expect and how to tackle the fences can make the difference between a winner and an also-ran!

Preparation

Walking the course is important. You must plan your route and know what types of fences there are. Your first impression of a jump is what the horse sees. If the fence looks like a jumble of poles to you, it will to the horse as well. Make a mental note of the aids your horse will need to jump clear.

Also think about the differences in light on the course when you go in and out of woods. Plan to take the route that gives your horse every chance of seeing what he has to do – by letting him have a good clear run up to each fence.

The ground varies too. On steep uphills aim to save your horse's strength.

▼ **Cross-country jumping** requires skill and intelligence from both horse and rider. Here the rider checks her pony's speed before dropping down to prevent jarring the legs or stumbling.

And save *yourself* on downhills by keeping in control!

Fences with a ditch

These range from a plain ditch – the trickiest to jump because most horses dislike coming upon a gaping hole – to trakehners and coffins.

Ditches with a fence behind are quite simple to jump – the fence distracts the horse's attention from the ditch. Take this type of fence at a reasonable pace and speed up over the last few strides. Steady and balance the horse about 12 strides away from the fence.

A trakehner is a suspended log or rail over a ditch. The rail can be set straight over the ditch or at an angle. Either way, jump the middle. Jumping to one side means you are left with a seemingly wide ditch and a stretch to clear the rail, or too much of an upright with all the ditch on the landing side.

Trakehners look imposing because the gap between the log and the ditch makes you think the fence is bigger than it is. If the fence looks too daunting, mentally fill in the ditch and the jump will appear to shrink.

Coffin: Any combination of rails and a ditch is called a coffin. The sequence is always rails-ditch-rails, but there can be either a stride or a bounce (no stride) between each element.

Keep the horse active but moving at a steady pace. He needs time to understand what he has to do and where to put his feet, but he must be bouncy enough to jump through the combination without stopping.

Fences with a level change

These take the form of a drop down, steps up or combine the two.

A drop fence is a jump from one level to a lower level. Slow down, because galloping off a drop either jars the horse's legs or makes him stumble on landing. Then slightly increase the pace in the last few strides. Lean back a little and let the reins slip through your hands to give the horse a free head. But don't have them so loose that there is a loop. You need your reins to help the pony keep his head up and keep his balance on landing.

Steps: Ride downward steps as you would a drop. When going up steps the horse needs to be moving eagerly, but collected enough for his hocks to be ➤

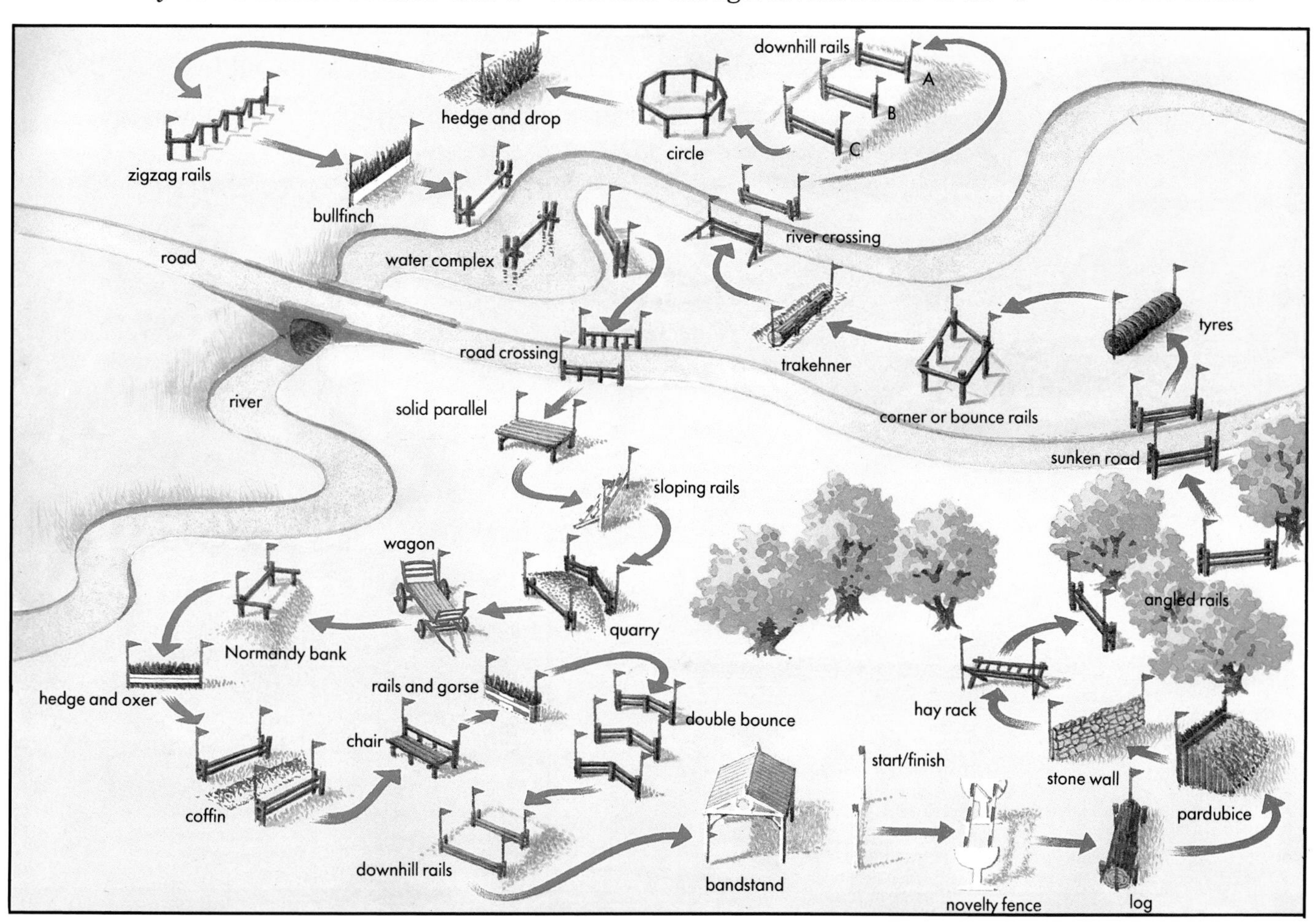

▼ **A sample of cross-country fences.** Courses vary from one competition to the next, but the type of jumps you meet are similar.

Tack across country

➤ **Grip reins** are best across country – even if it's wet and the reins are slippery, they won't run through your fingers.

A **breastplate** is advisable. It stops the saddle slipping back when the horse stretches for jumping and galloping.

Attached to the breastplate is a **running martingale**. This doesn't interfere with the horse, but keeps him from flinging his head up too high. Also use **rein stops** to prevent the martingale rings from catching the rein ends.

◄ **Brushing boots** protect the fetlocks if the horse knocks a fence, or strikes one leg with the other. Do them up so the pressure is even, with the fastenings to the outside and the straps pointing backward. **Overreach boots** are worn on the front feet. If your horse overreaches, his hindfeet may hit his forefeet and these boots prevent damage. Safest are pull-on rubber boots, as they are less likely to fall off than ones with fastenings.

➤ For safety, use a **leather girth**. A shaped girth is the most comfortable because it doesn't nip the horse's elbow.

As an extra precaution, fit a **surcingle**. This goes over the saddle and keeps it in position, even if the girth breaks. Always place the surcingle flat over the saddle and on top of the girth to prevent any pinching.

Check the stitching on your stirrup leathers before an event. Stirrup irons should be stainless steel for strength.

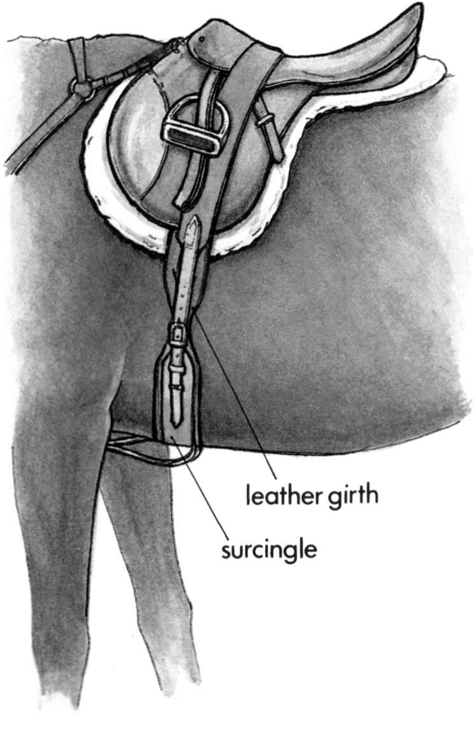

under him so he can bound up. Once up the first step, push on so that the horse keeps the momentum going.

Banks combine going up steps with a drop. Keep bounding forward to get a clean jump on to the bank, but don't come off too fast. A Normandy bank means a jump on to the bank and then a fence off; this needs a little more pace than a simple drop.

Combinations

Combination fences contain more than one element. They often include a series of obstacles through which you choose your route – the hardest routes are the fastest.

Go for the line that suits your horse's temperament *and* is safe and speedy. Walk every option beforehand. If you stop on the quick but difficult route and you haven't walked the easy way, you won't know where to go.

Water

The key to riding water fences is to go as slowly as possible but with enough impulsion to jump in and not stop. The faster you move the more likely the horse is to stumble – the drag effect of the water will bring him down. The same goes for riding out of the jump. The splashing can restrict the horse's vision and he will either stop or trip up at the bank.

▲ **Pony Club one-day events** are the best introduction to cross-country competitions. These two tackle the parallel rails eagerly, and the pony jumps big and clear.

◄ **Any level change** upward requires forward riding. The pony needs enough impetus to bound up to the top.

► **Slow up** before a drop fence. Lean back, otherwise you hit the pony's neck on landing. Let the reins slide through your fingers so the horse can stretch his head.

There are two aspects to consider when jumping a cross-country course – the speed at which you approach each fence and the route you take. You need to decide both when you are walking the course.

Bounce fence

A bounce fence consists of two fences positioned not more than a few metres from each other. A horse has to jump over the first fence, land in the middle and take off immediately for the second fence without a stride in between.

Approach with short, active strides. Keep the horse balanced and in a steady rhythm, but use your legs strongly to make sure that he is going forward with plenty of impulsion.

Solid fences

Solid fences such as stone walls may appear unnerving but horses usually jump them well as long as you give them enough confidence.

Approach: Aim straight toward the fence at a strong but even canter.

Slide-type fence

A slide-type fence consists of a jump at the top of a steep slide which leads to another fence a few paces from the bottom of the slope.

Approach at a steady pace. Going slowly gives the horse time to take in the ground-level changes but he must have enough speed to clear the fence at the top of the slide.

Settle yourself quickly after clearing the fence and sit up while going down the slide so that you are in a good position to apply the aids. Keep a rein contact and make the horse go forward with enough impulsion to negotiate the fence at the bottom.

False ground line

A ground line is 'false' when it is placed on the ground *behind* the top pole. False ground lines confuse horses as they make it difficult to judge the height of the fence.

Approach with a short, bouncy stride and strong leg so the horse can correct himself if he misjudges the fence.

◄ **This bullfinch fence is very high** but the top 60-90cm (2-3ft) of the brush is thin enough for the horse to jump through. The ditch in front provides a good ground line.

★ **BETWEEN THE FLAGS**

Red and white flags are placed at the sides of each fence. You have to ride between these flags – the red flag must be on your right and the white flag on your left.

▼ **Stone walls** can look dauntingly solid. Make sure your horse can see that there's ground the other side and ride with confidence so he trusts you.

Here at the Pony Club Championships, Lara Barnett approaches the jump head on to give her horse the best opportunity of clearing it successfully.

➤ **Fences with roofs** come in all shapes and sizes. This jump is set in a stone tunnel. The horse may find the roof distracting, so coax his attention away from it by riding confidently.

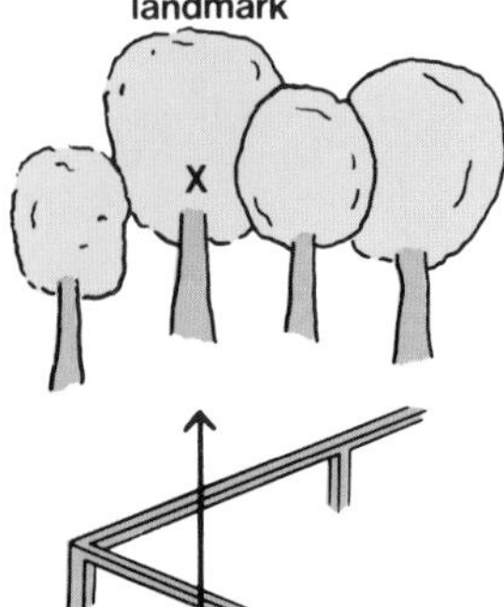

← 1m →

route over corner

▼ ▲ **If you decide to take the corner,** draw an imaginary straight line about 1m (3ft) from the corner – so that both the front and the back rails are at an equal angle. Look out for a clear landmark which continues the straight line and link up these three points so that you arrive at the fence straight.

Corner fence

A corner fence consists of two upright fences at angles to each other and forming a point where they join. It is fastest to jump straight over the corner, but more cautious to take each fence either as a bounce or with a stride or two in between.

If you decide to take the corner in one, look out for a clear landmark (like a tree or telegraph pole) in the distance. When approaching the fence line up with this landmark and keep your eyes on it all the time. This helps you to arrive at the fence straight. Once the horse has taken off from the correct point he can stretch over the fence to clear it.

Approach: Steady and balance the horse, then approach. Find your line as soon as you are on course and ride strongly into it.

Fence with a roof

Some horses don't notice the roof on covered fences, especially if the 'hat' is high.

Approach: Ride strongly so that the horse concentrates on the jump itself. If he is unsure, he may duck at the last minute causing either a fall or refusal – particularly if he has not seen this type of fence before.

Fence sizes at novice level

In all events affiliated to the British Horse Trials Association, there are maximum heights and widths for cross-country fences at each level – novice, intermediate and advanced. At novice level the maximum height is 1.08m (3ft 6in). Other key sizes for novice fences are:

Spread with height	
Maximum spread at top	1.2m (3ft 11in)
Maximum spread at base	2.1m (6ft 11in)
Spread only	
Maximum spread – dry ditch	2.74m (9ft)
Maximum spread – water	3.05m (10ft)
Drop fences	
Maximum drop	1.6m (5ft 3in)
Jump into water	
Maximum depth of water	0.3m (1ft)

A corner fence

There are three ways of tackling this corner fence and you must decide on your route when walking the course. Jumping the corner (**A**) is usually quickest. The risk of running out is greater on a corner, so only take this approach if your horse jumps straight.

If you feel this route is too tricky, take the jump in two parts as a bounce fence (**B**) – but you need an athletic horse. Safer still but slower, you can take a few strides between each fence (**C**). This is probably the best route if you are at all unsure – remember that two or three time penalties are better than 20 jumping penalties.

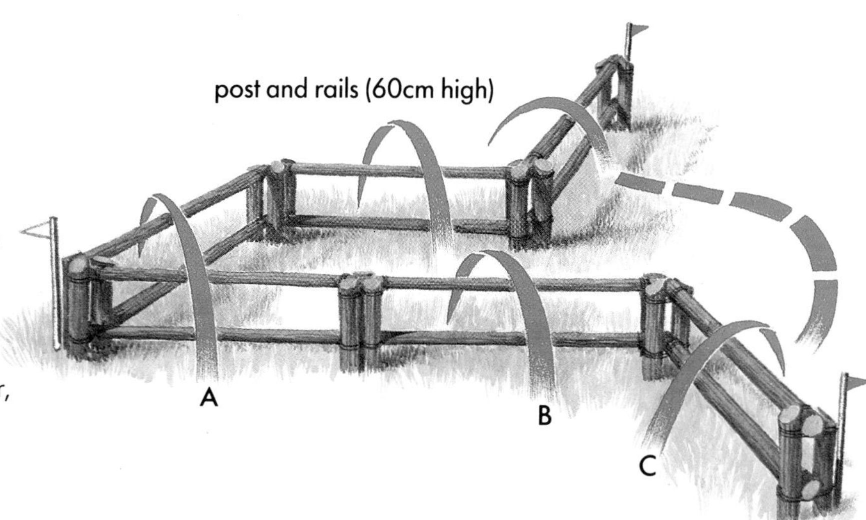

A water combination

This water combination offers two alternative routes. The fastest line is straight through the middle (**A**), but this involves two tricky fences – a drop fence into water and a step-up bank at the other side. The easier but slower way (**B**) takes you down the gentle slope into the water, with time when you come out to re-balance before jumping.

post and rails (45cm high)

step up bank (30cm high)

slope into water

suspended plank (45cm high)

upright rails (60cm high)

post and rails (60cm high)

B

A

Thorough preparation at home gives you a chance of success once you reach the competition stage. This partnership is tackling a triple combination in the jumping arena at the National Schools and Pony Club Jumping Championships at Hickstead.

Jumping combinations

When you have practised jumping combinations at home, and perhaps had a go in one or two novice classes at local shows, you should feel ready to move on to the next stage.

Course design

A good course builder tries to design a show-jumping course that challenges the rider without upsetting the pony. He follows some basic guidelines as to distances. This is helpful in training as you can prepare at home for the sort of tests you will meet at shows.

It helps to know how a pony jumps and lands over each type of obstacle:

Upright fence: Take off and landing should be the height of the jump away from the jump.

Parallel fence: Take off is slightly closer than for an upright, so the pony's highest point is nearer the back rail. Landing is farther away than for an upright.

Staircase fence: Take off is even closer and landing farther away than for a parallel. This is often the easiest type of fence to jump.

Try varying the type of fence you use in combinations and remember that sometimes you need to change the distances between the two parts. For example, a spread followed by an upright needs more room than a spread followed by another spread. Keep this in mind when you walk a jumping course.

▼ **Cross-country combinations** test the horse's stamina and 'handiness' – it isn't just a case of gallop and jump and hope for the best!

Open classes

If your pony has been successful over small courses, and is jumping with confidence, you might think about entering him in Open classes.

The recommended distances for a double with one non-jumping stride (measured from fence to fence, not landing to take off) for pony Open classes are: under 12.2 hands high, 6.1–7.3m (20–24ft); 12.2–13.2 hands high, 6.4–7.6m (21–25ft); 13.2–14.2 hands high, 6.7–7.9m (22–26ft).

It is very important not to rush and overface yourself or your pony. At the same time, if you want to compete you must set yourself targets – raise the jumps and then stretch out the distances a little at a time.

When you reach this stage, you must be confident and be able to ride with plenty of thought and determination.

Training for cross country

Show jumping is not the only possibility for the jumping enthusiast. You may enjoy riding cross country and want to enter one-day events and hunter trials.

Preparation is all-important. It is never too soon to teach your pony to cope with varying ground conditions and hills. Encourage him to keep the same rhythm and speed going up and down hills – no rushing or plunging down or pausing before making an upward climb! And no more walking round puddles!

If possible, make some cross-country fences at home to practise over. For example, you could dig a small ditch,

▲ **Ditches** can be off-putting for novice ponies and riders. There is no need for this if you learn sensibly. The first ditch you attempt should be small enough to step over so your pony can learn that a 'hole in the ground' is not a disguised snake pit! Following a lead also helps give your pony confidence.

Hold the mane the first time in case your pony takes a big leap. Don't rush at ditches before he is used to them, but equally don't stop every time to let him have a good look or he may decide not to go at all. Wide ditches are never as bad as they seem if you remember that a single canter stride is about 3m (10ft) long!

then make a bank out of the diggings. Use sleepers to make a 'box' for the spare soil, about the same width as a normal jump and flat on top.

The bank can be used for all kinds of combinations. If you can, make room for a canter stride on top, jump on and off, then follow with a low fence one stride later. This can be jumped from either direction. Try putting the jump right up to the drop off the bank so that you can make your first 'drop' fence, with the take off higher than the landing.

This sort of work teaches your pony to be clever on his feet, and can be great fun for both of you. Look for natural obstacles when you are out hacking – fallen trees or small ditches. As with show jumping, the key to success is to aim for variety before height.

Bounces and angles

'Bounce' fences are combinations *without* a non-jumping stride in between. They are never used in show jumping, but often in cross country.

Your experience with doubles will tell you how to space the jump – the bigger the jump, the longer the distance to use. The faster you go, the longer your pony's

▲ ► **Cross-country obstacles** include ditches, banks, water and drop fences – and any mixture that makes challenging combinations.

You will need to alter your position a little to suit each type of fence – for example, you sit more upright for the drop fences before landing. Studying photographs of people jumping cross country in three-day events can give you a better idea of when to sit back and when to stay forward.

stride and, again, the greater the distance you need.

Sometimes it helps to be able to jump at an angle. Angled poles often appear in hunter trials. They are usually a quicker option through a combination when you are riding against the clock. Don't make your angle too steep or you may go past the jump altogether!

It is much harder to keep your pony 'between leg and hand' on this kind of approach, so it's well worth practising. It improves your riding enormously. This is also a good time to try short approaches to obstacles - using smaller, easy fences at first.

Keep your eyes and ears open for new ideas and you'll find that, even with few facilities at home, you and your pony can soon become a skilful partnership.

◄ **The fastest route** in the cross country is over a corner and to negotiate this needs bold, accurate riding.

▼ **Bounce fences** are a common feature of cross-country courses. Always tackle this type of combination slowly and with impulsion.

Cross-country problems

◄**Successful** cross-country jumping takes many years of training. You must teach your horse to trust you and meet every challenge with confidence. When he jumps a course clear, you'll know that all your hard work has paid off.

Every cross-country rider experiences problems from time to time. Ponies often become over-excited before starting the event, some hate water fences, while others run out of steam before they have completed the course.

Confidence and trust

Confidence is all-important in cross-country riding. A pony must feel completely sure that his rider won't ask him to jump a fence that is dangerous or likely to cause him any harm.

This trust is gained by years of patient training. Thorough schooling on the flat improves your pony's balance and agility. Never ask too much of your pony too soon. He must be introduced gradually to all the hazards he is likely to meet. If you ask him to try something too difficult, he may suddenly panic and decide he can't cope. Remember always to reward your pony when he is brave enough to trust you and meet whatever challenge you have demanded of him.

Q

I never know what to look out for when I walk a cross-country course. Have you any tips?

A

One of the keys to successful jumping is getting the right approach for each fence. As you walk the course, go over the fences in your own mind, and picture yourself approaching each jump.

Pick a landmark such as a tree to help you line up the fence and plan how you'll ride it. Always take a line which jumps the fence straight and in the middle. If you're not sure how to ride a fence, ask an experienced rider.

Where there is more than one possible approach to a fence, always walk the various options so that if you have a problem jumping the direct way, you can tackle it by an easier route at the second attempt. Sometimes it's better to play safe and opt for the longer, less demanding route – a few time penalties are better than the penalties for a refusal.

Concentration is vital when walking the course. Walk it on your own and think about each fence carefully before moving to the next.

Q

Before the start of a cross-country event my pony becomes very excited. How can I calm him down?

A

A pony soon learns to associate the starter's countdown with the excitement of the cross-country course and he may suffer from as many nerves as his rider. To keep your pony relaxed, pat and reassure him as much as possible and try not to shorten the reins – this is a signal for him to start.

Walk or jog him round very quietly on a long rein if possible and take him into the starting box at the last moment only. Keep relaxed yourself by taking a few deep breaths – your nervousness transmits itself easily to your pony. The trick is to bluff him into thinking that it's not his turn to go.

Q

My pony hates getting his feet wet and refuses to tackle water jumps. How can I teach him to jump into water?

A

It is a natural reaction for horses and ponies to be wary of water, especially when they don't know how deep it is. In the wild, horses go to the water's edge to drink but never venture further in.

You have to teach a pony to trust you. A young pony should be walked through as many puddles as possible so that he becomes used to getting his feet wet. Once he is quite confident about puddles, he can be asked to splash through streams. If he's reluctant to cross a stream, ask a friend with a more confident horse to give you a lead.

Ride with determination, but at the same time try to make the whole exercise fun for the pony. Encourage him to splash and sniff the water. If possible, trot and canter through puddles and larger expanses of water – checking carefully first that the bottom is safe.

Eventually your pony will learn to trust you and go into any water when you ask him. Bring him through water regularly to remind him that there is nothing to be frightened of and that it can even be fun.

Q

I'm a bit nervous of drop fences: my pony often leaves me behind and then I accidentally catch him in the mouth. What is the best way to tackle fences like this?

A

Once you know the technique for tackling drop fences they become less daunting. The most important point to remember is your position. When approaching a drop, you should keep your pony strongly between hand and leg. Once he has taken off, keep your head up. This ensures your shoulders stay back. You must put your weight firmly in your heel and keep your lower leg well forward on landing. The lower leg acts as a brace to support the upper body.

Your balance is vital when tackling drops. To maintain your balance, keep your weight further back when you land. This helps the pony maintain *his* balance and puts you in a secure position to ride confidently forward to the next fence.

Q

My pony often seems to run out of energy toward the end of the cross-country course. Is there anything I can do to help him?

A

Eventing is a demanding sport and both pony and rider must be fit.

Cross-country courses for ponies are quite short and your pony should be able to cope without showing signs of tiredness. You must give him time to reach eventing fitness before you consider entering him for a competition. If he tires toward the end of a course, keep a strong contact on the reins and your legs firmly on his sides. This supports him and gives him extra energy.

Cross-country fences

◀ **Although a ditch** in front of a fence looks daunting to the rider, it acts as a natural ground line for the horse and makes it easier for him to judge his take-off point.

★ **KNOW YOUR FLAGS**
On the cross-country phase of events, each fence is marked with a red and a white flag. You must jump between the flags, keeping the red flag on your right and the white on your left.

The cross-country phase of one-day and three-day events is the most challenging of the competition. There are a number of standard cross-country fences that appear regularly in events. Knowing how to tackle them means you and your horse can compete confidently on the day.

Option fences

An option fence gives the rider a choice of ways to jump. There is always a long, slow route and a short, fast way that is more difficult to jump. You must decide which way is more suitable for the experience of both yourself and your horse. Some people call the long way the 'chicken route' – but there's nothing chicken about it! It is often far more sensible to ride the long way and show your horse some thought if he isn't up to it.

A corner fence is a typical option – you can jump each part separately or both elements together where they meet at the corner. To do it in one go, the horse must jump a corner absolutely straight, otherwise he risks running out or jumping a part of the fence which is too wide. A corner should be tackled only by an experienced combination of horse and rider, and certainly not by the nervous.

If you feel confident enough to give it a try, concentrate on your line of approach. Find a landmark beyond the line you wish to take and look toward that. The line should be as near to the narrowest part of the corner as possible. Rhythm, balance, impulsion, plus accuracy of approach are all vital for jumping a corner successfully.

Option fence

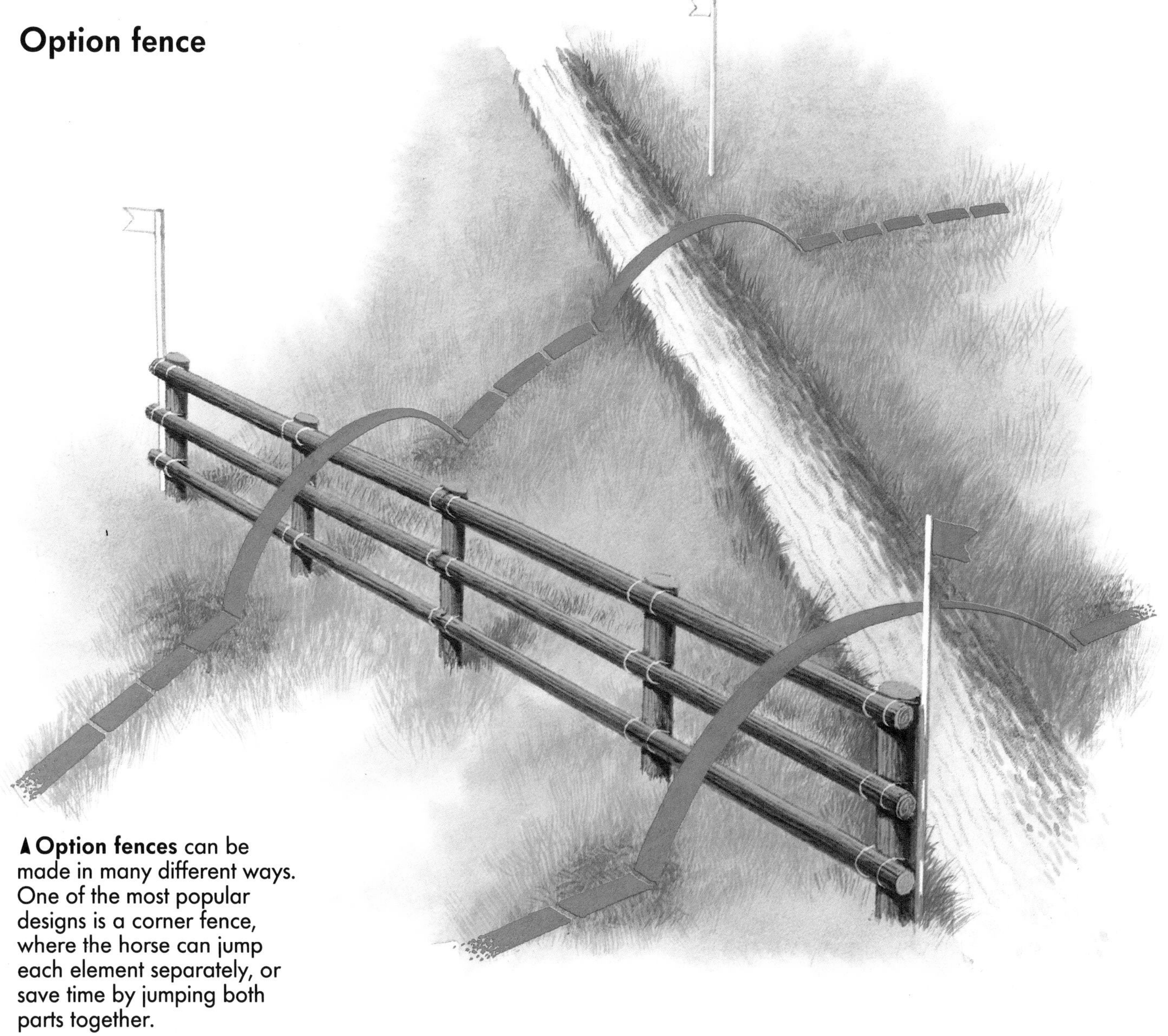

▲ **Option fences** can be made in many different ways. One of the most popular designs is a corner fence, where the horse can jump each element separately, or save time by jumping both parts together.

Ditch

▲A ditch on the landing side of a fence poses a problem for the horse as he is unaware that it's there until he's in mid-air. He must be encouraged to take an extra-big jump.

Riders tend to be intimidated by fences with ditches on the take-off side. In fact, these ditches help to give the horse a take-off line, and prevent him getting too close to the fence before he jumps. Don't allow the horse to look down into the ditch or he might take fright. Ride to the fence in a positive, confident manner to encourage him to adopt the same attitude. Nervousness on your part is transmitted to the horse.

A ditch on the landing side of a fence is a hidden hazard. The horse is unaware that it's there, so it is up to you to tell him to make a bigger effort. A slight increase in pace helps the horse find the energy to make the spread of the fence and the ditch behind.

Coffin

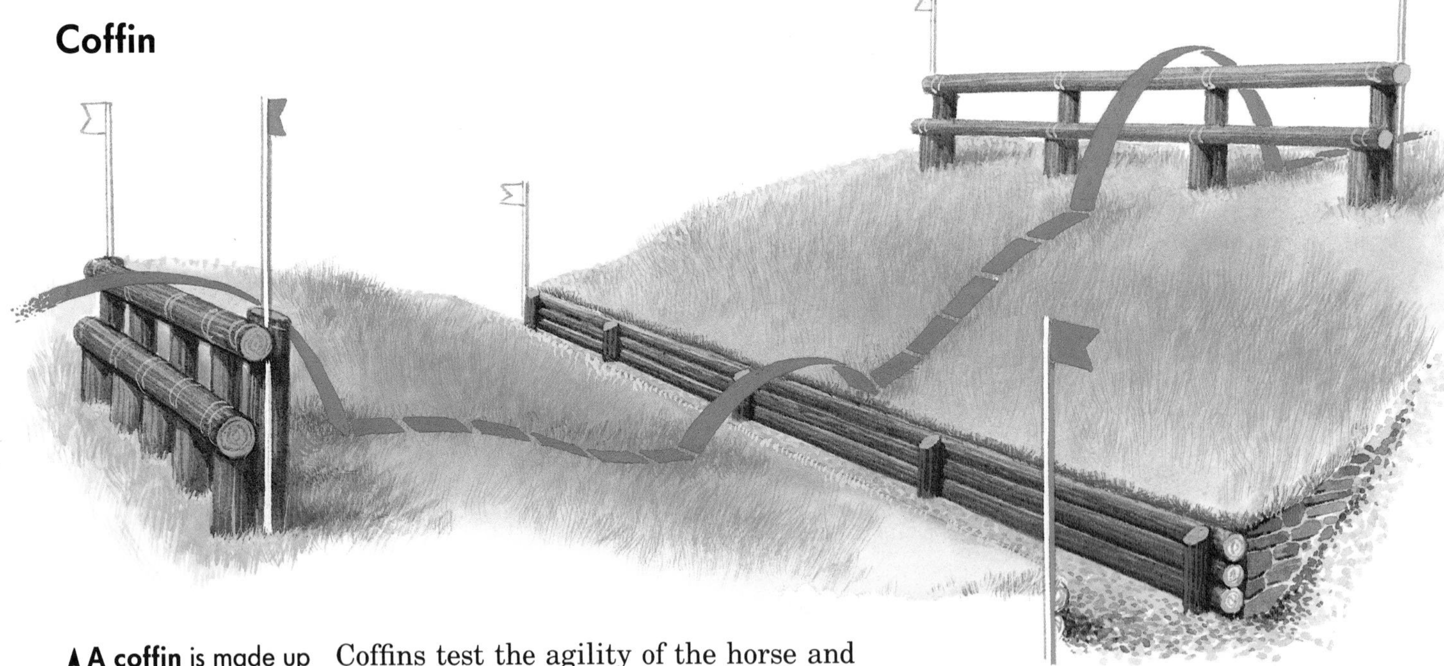

▲A coffin is made up of two fences with a ditch between them. The horse usually has to jump a fence, take a stride and jump the ditch, then take another stride before clearing the other fence.

Coffins test the agility of the horse and the courage of both horse and rider.

A coffin involves a combination of fences and a ditch. The traditional coffin is an upright rail to a ditch, followed by another upright rail. These are normally one stride apart, but the distances can vary from a bounce to two strides. The ground in between may be flat, but the middle element is sometimes placed lower, making it much more difficult to jump successfully.

Approach a coffin with plenty of impulsion on a short bouncy stride. If the pace on the approach is too fast, the horse may worry that he is going to jump straight into the ditch. Ride strongly through the combination, but without allowing the horse to fall on to his forehand. Don't drop the contact before the horse has taken off, otherwise you could risk a refusal. If you keep an even rhythm, you'll find it easier to cope with this kind of combination fence.

To jump coffins your horse must have faith in you. He must know that he is approaching the fence in a safe, positive manner and that there is no danger of him landing in the bottom of the ditch and hurting himself.

Uphill jump

There are many types of uphill fence – one popular jump with course builders is a bank followed by a fence on a slope.

Exactly the same principles apply for jumping an uphill fence as for other fences: rhythm, balance and impulsion. The horse automatically uses his hocks more when he goes uphill, but you must still ride strongly to maintain enough impulsion to jump the fence.

Although you're going uphill, don't lean too far forward – this puts too much weight on the horse's forehand and makes it difficult for him to lift himself over the fence. Keep your head up and shoulders back. Lean forward only when the horse lifts his front legs off the ground. In this way, balance and rhythm are preserved and the horse is given as much help as possible to jump.

▲ **Fences built on a slope** can be designed in many different ways. They often include a bank and then a fence with a slight drop on the landing side. You need plenty of impulsion to clear both obstacles.

Bounce fence

A bounce involves two obstacles with no stride between them. The horse jumps the first element and must immediately take off for the second. A double bounce has three separate fences, all 4-5m (13-16ft) apart, so the horse has to jump three times without taking a stride in between the fences.

The fences vary from rails and palisades (stakes bound together) to logs. Bounce spreads are found only in advanced cross-country courses.

The approach for a bounce fence is much the same as for a coffin. It must be a controlled, bouncy pace with plenty of impulsion but not speed. Sit up on the approach and keep your shoulders back – this helps the horse stay on his hocks and not drop on to his forehand. If the horse has too much weight on his forehand, he'll be unable to jump the second and third elements. Maintain a firm contact throughout the combination to help the horse. Sit up in between elements, to keep him on his hocks.

▲ **A bounce combination** consists of two or three fences without a stride between them. The horse jumps, lands and jumps again immediately. The fences can be placed on level ground or on a slope, which makes them more difficult to tackle.

Cross-country problems: 2

Although every cross-country fence should be approached with impulsion, rhythm and balance, some fences pose problems all of their own.

Road to success

Much of the challenge of cross-country riding is knowing how to tackle the range of fences you come across at a competition. The approach differs from obstacle to obstacle, and this demands great skill from both horse and rider.

Some horses have problems with particular fences – an option is troublesome for a pony who can't turn easily, for instance. Jumping big is a problem that other riders can meet at nearly any fence. Careful preparation can do much to instil confidence in horse and rider to avoid mistakes.

▼ **A bold, confident horse** is the product of thorough training on the flat as well as over fences. His performance also depends on your faith in him. A horse's attitude to any obstacle hangs on his rider's ability and courage.

My pony jumps quite big over his fences. I often feel insecure and lose a stirrup. Why does this happen and how can I improve my position?

A

First of all, remember that it is much better to have a pony who is keen to jump – even if it means he is a little difficult to sit on sometimes – than one who is reluctant. Many ponies become very excited during a cross-country course and it is only natural for an enthusiastic pony to fight for his head and tackle the fences with gusto.

Careful schooling on the flat, making sure your pony listens to your aids, helps you to control him on the cross-country course and helps him to jump with more economy. Practise over small jumps until your confidence has improved.

Learn to go with your pony when he jumps big. If your heel comes up, it pushes your weight up and forward and you lose your balance. Keep your heels down to secure your leg and seat position. Avoid getting in front of or behind the movement. Always wait until your pony takes off before you lean forward – in this way you are ready for hesitation or an unexpected reaction from him.

You could try strengthening your seat by riding without stirrups. Get an instructor to give you lessons on the lunge – she can show you leg exercises to improve your position. Alternatively ride standing up in your stirrups – this tests your balance, strengthens the muscles of your legs and also helps to make your ankles more supple by exercising the muscles round them.

Q

What is the best way of tackling steps?

A

Steps are unnatural obstacles for a horse to jump. He needs to learn how to cope with them.

The horse should approach upward steps with plenty of impulsion. The pace should be quite slow otherwise he doesn't have time to land and push off again. It is all too easy for him to lose energy when jumping up a series of steps, so you must work hard to maintain the impulsion.

Downward steps are generally easier, but you have to concentrate on keeping your position and staying balanced. Approach in a bouncy canter – you could drop into a trot just before jumping. Maintain the impulsion, otherwise you risk a refusal. The more rhythm you have when jumping down, the easier it is to keep your position. Keep your weight in your heels and your lower legs slightly forward so that you can brace against the stirrup. Keep your upper body just behind the movement and look ahead.

Q

My pony is hard to turn, particularly after a fence. This makes options difficult to tackle. How can I improve my control over him?

A

Most ponies become stronger when jumping and the speed of cross country exposes any flaws in their flatwork training. Until you can canter and turn without heaving and hauling your pony, you cannot expect him to jump and turn comfortably.

Return to work on the flat and practise your turns. Only when you have perfected your training should you have another go at jumping.

You may also need to change the type of bit you're using. Don't put your pony in a severe bit, however, until you have asked your instructor for advice.

Q

My pony hates jumping into woods. How can I convince him that he will come to no harm?

A

Jumping into woods can frighten a pony for many reasons. Going from light to shade with little time to adjust his eyes is a common fear for a pony approaching this jump.

When you walk the cross-country course before the competition, carefully plan the route that gives your pony the best view of what is ahead of him and what he has to do. Work out a good clear run up to the fence.

During the competition, approach the fence with plenty of impulsion, but not too quickly. This gives the pony time to assess the situation, to see that there is nothing frightening, and have the energy to jump clear.

Ride strongly and stay in balance with your pony to convince him that you are confident and he has no cause for worry – he could be fretting about hitting a tree, for instance.

Q

Which is the best way to jump trakehner fences? I find them rather frightening.

Any fence with a ditch underneath gives the impression of being much bigger than it actually is. The skill of the course builder is to frighten the riders when they walk the course, but at the same time to make the fences jumpable for the horses.

Quite often a ditch underneath a fence creates a ground line for the horse and prevents him getting too close for take off. For this to work, the horse mustn't be allowed to look into the ditch or he may miss his stride. You shouldn't look into it either – remember you tend to land wherever you look.

Approach a trakehner in a strong canter and pretend to yourself that the ditch doesn't exist – if you start worrying about it, your nervousness will be conveyed to your horse.

If the log over the ditch is set at an angle, jump the ditch straight and the rail at an angle. Jumping the ditch at an angle gives a false impression of its width and can all too easily lead to your horse falling into it on the landing side.

Trakehners can be frightening, so they must be negotiated with confidence. Plenty of practice over small ditches and rails should help you and your horse master the specialized jumping method required for these obstacles and give you the confidence you need.

Eventing: show jumping

➤ **In a three-day event,** the show jumping competition is held the day after the gruelling speed and endurance phase and is a real test of the horse's obedience, suppleness and fitness.

The show-jumping phase of eventing tests the horse's obedience, suppleness and fitness – particularly in three-day events when it comes after the rigours of the cross country.

Change of order

The order of phases for three-day events is dressage, speed and endurance (cross country) and, on the third day, show jumping. If the show jumping took place after the cross country on the same day, the horse would be tired and stiff. At the same time, the thrill of the cross country would leave him too excited for the discipline of jumping in an arena.

In one and two-day events, however, the show-jumping phase usually comes between dressage and cross country. It is easier for horse and rider to perform a good show-jumping round after the dressage phase. The horse is relaxed and obedient with his hocks underneath his body – ready both mentally and physically for accurate jumping.

In three-day events there is a veterinary inspection on the final day before the show jumping. This is to check that all the horses are fit and sound enough to complete the competition. The inspection does not take place in one and two-day events.

▼ **The order of the three phases** depends on the type of event. In one and two-day events, dressage comes first, show jumping second and cross country last. In three-day events, dressage is held on the first day, speed and endurance on the second, and show jumping on the final day.

Training for the jumping phase should run hand in hand with flat work for the dressage – the better-schooled your pony is on the flat, the better his jumping will be.

Dressage

Cross country

Show jumping

What the phase tests

At affiliated level, events are organized by the British Horse Trials Association, and pure show jumping by the British Show Jumping Association. The penalty systems reflect the different qualities expected of eventing horses and show-jumping horses. Knowing how you are penalized helps you understand what is required when you take part in an event at any level.

An event horse must at all costs be bold, so he is severely penalized if he refuses (10 points), but for knocking down a fence he receives only half the number of faults (five points). He must also be quick thinking and agile enough to get out of tricky situations, so a fall of horse and/or rider incurs a hefty 30 penalties.

In pure show jumping, the fences are much larger to test the specialized skill of the horse. If a horse reaches one of these enormous fences at a take-off point which makes jumping the fence impossible (without crashing through it), it is better that he refuses than injures himself or his rider. As a result, a show jumper is penalized much less than the eventing horse for refusing a fence (three faults), while knocking down a jump is more serious (four faults).

There is normally a jump off to decide the winner in BSJA show jumping. In eventing, the competitor jumps only one round, because the faults are added to the penalty scores from the dressage and cross-country phases.

In three-day-event show jumping, the horses jump in reverse order of merit. This puts more pressure on the rider to have a good round, as faults are costly when you're trying to retain your overnight position after the cross country. 'Surprise' wins by competitors low in the placings after the cross country, who then go on to complete a faultless show-jumping round, happen more often than you might think.

▼ **The fences** are relatively small compared to those found in pure show jumping. But the event horse is expected to be courageous, so he is heavily penalized if he refuses.

Training

There is no secret to producing a pony who jumps smooth, rhythmical clear rounds. It is a matter of hard work, patience, and time spent training both you and your pony.

In eventing, as in any competitive riding, the importance lies in having a well-schooled pony, versatile enough to perform a dressage test, jump safely at speed on the cross country, and carefully in the show jumping. Your job is to train the pony so that he can cope with all three disciplines – he must be supple, fit and obedient to the aids.

Most riders need help doing this – whatever their level of ability. When schooling horses either on the flat or over fences, it is extremely helpful to have someone 'on the ground'. They can actually *see* what is going wrong – it's not always possible for the rider to feel the problem.

By the time a pony is competing in novice events, he should have had a thorough grounding. Even though he is not familiar with the arena, he should be quite happy and confident about the size of obstacle he is being asked to jump. After that, it is up to the rider to prepare carefully and know how best to tackle the course.

▼ **Training is the key to success** in eventing, which involves a lot of hard work for both you and the pony.

This three-year-old – being lunged Australian style – is in the very early stages of his training.

Mark Todd, who won the individual gold medal at two successive Olympic Games, on Charisma. Charisma was a highly successful event horse but on occasion dropped down in the placings due to a moment's carelessness in the show-jumping phase.

Don't underestimate the influence of the show-jumping phase – many a prestigious three-day event has been won or lost on the strength of it. It is important to produce a clear round in the show jumping because the final scores after the dressage and cross-country phases are often extremely close.

The course design

The course builder designs a show-jumping course for eventing differently from one for pure show jumping. He makes the route flow more easily than a BSJA track of a similar size.

There are fewer doubles and triples, so horse and rider have less related distances and stride lengths to worry about. The fences are solidly built (but may include a water jump at Intermediate or Advanced level).

On the other hand, every phase in eventing takes place outside – whatever the weather. The going can be deep, heavy or slippery, which puts extra demands on the training of the event horse. He must cope with any conditions – and really use his hocks for jumping.

Walking the course

It is up to the rider to walk the course so that he or she can ride it correctly. If possible, it is best to walk the course twice. Your first walk round gives you a general idea of the course, the turns into the fences and the distances in the doubles. It is important not to ride the turns too wide or you might get time faults.

The second walk should be an imaginary 'ride' round the course – pretend you are actually on your pony. This makes it much easier when it comes to riding the course for real, as it feels like the second

▼ **A sample show-jumping course** for eventing – Intermediate or Advanced (there is no water jump in Novice or Junior classes). The course is designed to be more flowing and less demanding than pure show jumping.

The practice fences must not exceed the height on the course, and are jumped in one direction only.

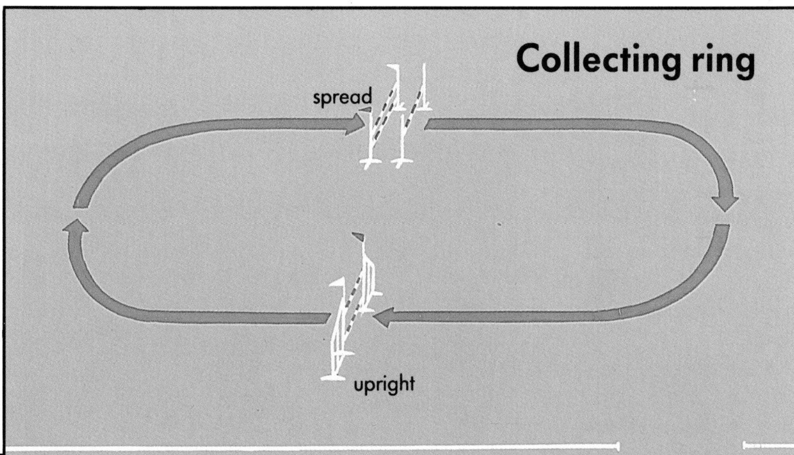

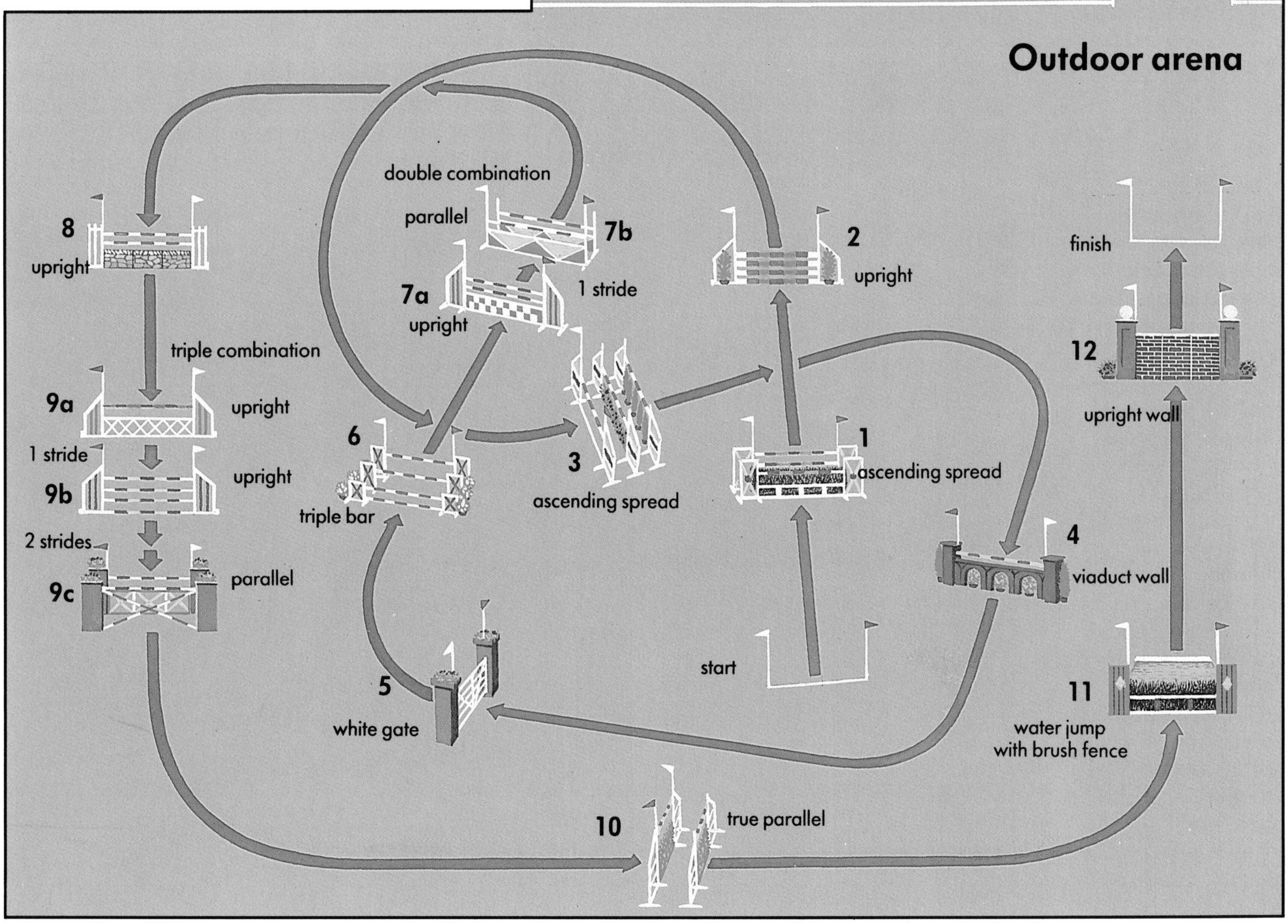

▲ **The final adjustments:** Make sure you leave a few minutes to change your clothes and tidy yourself up between phases.

time around. Show jumping is never easy but preparing yourself and your pony as thoroughly as possible helps enormously.

Warming up

At a one-day event, the pony has already performed his dressage test before the show jumping. This means he has had at least three quarters of an hour's work, so unless your pony is very difficult to settle, you need about 20 minutes of riding in before you jump.

Use the time to get your pony moving forward from his hocks and working in a rhythmical, balanced way. Circles, transitions and changes of direction help achieve this.

Once you feel that he is supple and obedient, you can start to use the practice fences. It is a good idea to trot over a low cross-pole and then canter over an upright, before moving on to a spread fence.

The rules state that it is forbidden to jump a fence in the practice ring which is higher than the maximum height allowed for the course. It is also against the rules to use a placing pole in front of the fence, although you are permitted to use a ground line.

Take note of the flags on the practice fences and jump them in the indicated direction only – red flag on the right and white flag on the left. Make sure you follow these rules when using the practice ring – you are sharing it with several other competitors.

➤ **Walk the course twice** if possible. This ingrains it in your memory, and so reduces the chance of your taking the wrong track.

Take note of the position of the start and finish, and listen out for the sound of the bell so you know what to expect as the starting signal.

Three-day event

At a three-day event, your pony should have a good night's rest after his cross-country round. A trot up in-hand in the early evening indicates how stiff or sore he is likely to be in the morning. He must pass a veterinary inspection next day, before going in for the show-jumping section.

Trot him up again first thing on the show-jumping day – walk off any stiffness by leading him in-hand or taking him for a gentle ride. It is best to keep the pony on the move until his turn to be presented to the veterinary panel, so

➤ **The amount of time** you spend riding in before the show jumping depends on the type of event. At a one-day event the show jumping comes after the dressage. Your pony should already be warmed up and won't need much more than 15 or 20 minutes' work, including jumping the practice fences.

The pony needs more warming up at a three-day event because he is likely to be stiff from the day before. Not too much though – he'll also be quite tired.

◄ ▲ **The horse should always** wear boots when jumping, to avoid injury.

In eventing the only type of martingale you are allowed to use is a running one.

plan your timing carefully.

The pony will probably need more loosening up than at a one-day event. However, as he is likely to be rather tired, it is important not to work him more than necessary. He will be less athletic than normal and his reactions may be slower. Even if he is a little tired and his muscles ache, however, it will not harm him to do one round of show jumping.

Dressage with fences

When your turn comes, try not to feel nervous as this is when errors occur. Be doubly sure about the course, wait for the bell, then ride with rhythm and balance firmly in mind. Remember where to turn – not too wide, but not cutting the corners – and don't forget to ride through the finish!

The show-jumping phase is a vital part of an event and should be thought of as being dressage with fences. In fact, dressage, show jumping and cross country should always be thought of as variations on the same theme and not as separate, different disciplines. Remember that and both you and your pony will enjoy safe, successful eventing.

▼ **The show-jumping phase** is extremely important and your pony must be happy to go over all types of fences!

The scores at this stage are often close. Five penalties or even a time fault may be the deciding margin – and you want it to be in your favour!

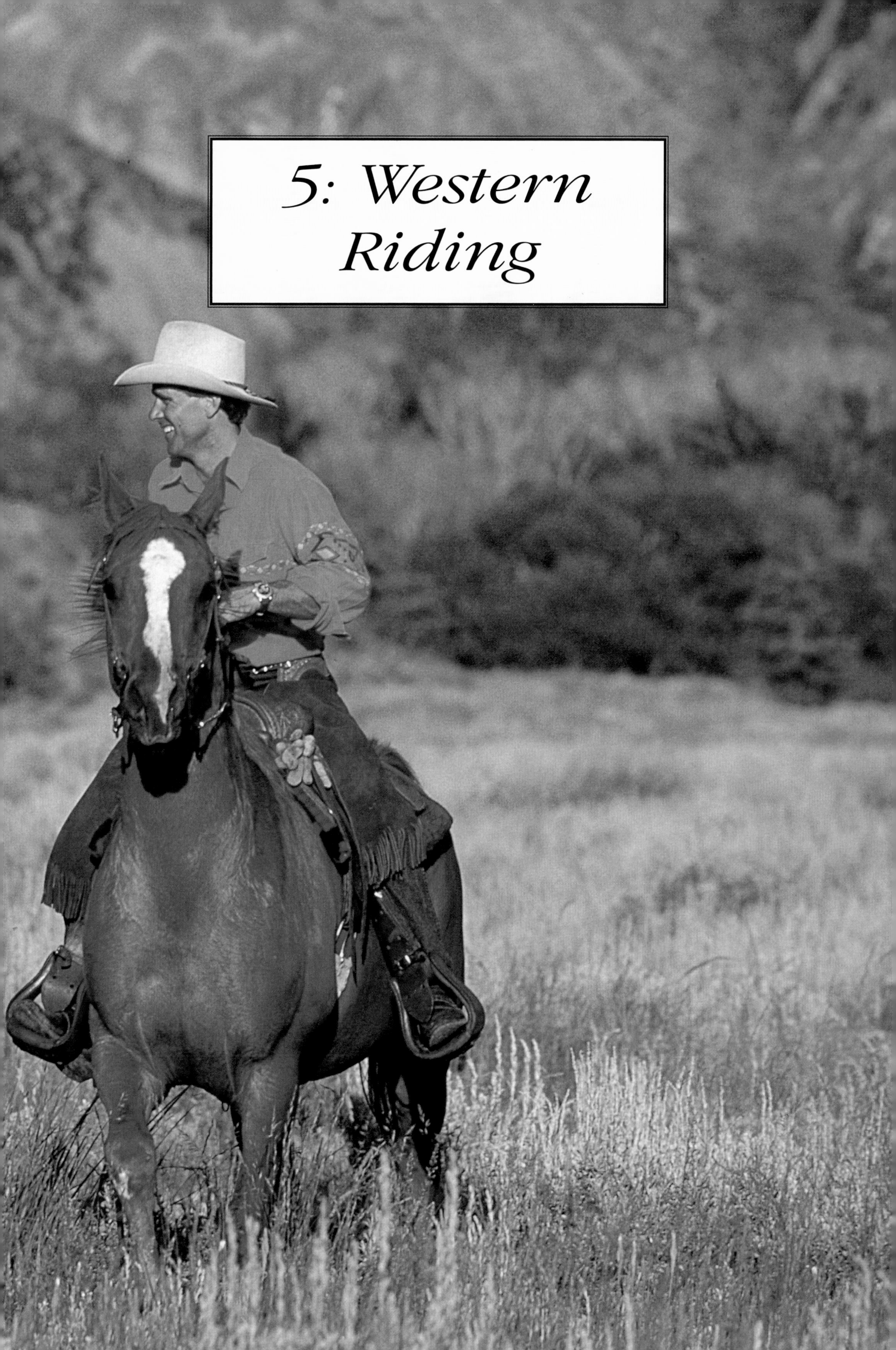

5: Western Riding

First Western riding lesson

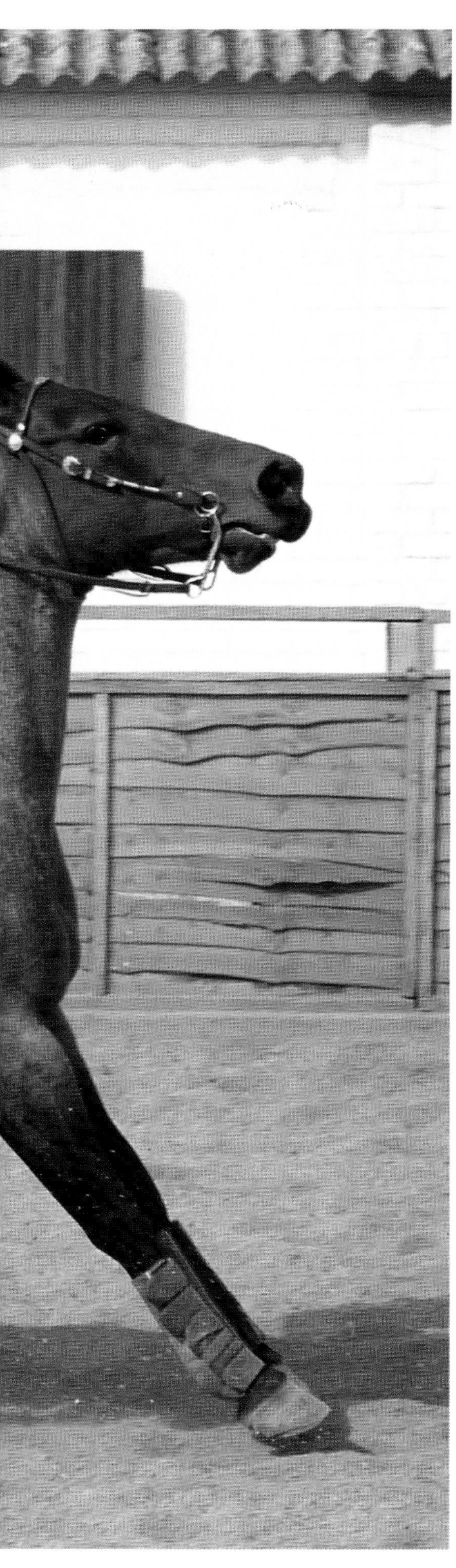

Western riding is traditionally associated with cowboys. It is a working form of riding developed in southern America to make the job of cattle raising over open plains easier. A Western rider works with a loose rein contact and gives the minimum of signals to the horse.

The background

Western riding was introduced to America over 400 years ago when Spaniards invaded the American continent. They brought with them their expertise in horsemanship which the Americans learned and adapted to suit their needs.

Nowadays Western riding is practised by riders all over the world. Many horses are trained to perform Western skills even though some never work cattle. They are taught to display their abilities in the show ring, on long-distance rides and sometimes just for pleasure.

Western requirements

Like a dressage horse, a Western mount must be athletic, intelligent and obedient. It also needs to be fairly small, so that it can perform the difficult turns and movements needed for cattle work – about 15.2 hands high is the maximum. The Quarter horse is one of the most popular Western breeds.

◄ ▼ **The roots** of Western and classical riding are the same but the techniques differ. The sliding stop (left) and neck reining (below) – which leaves one hand free – suit the work of cattle raising.

◄ **The sliding stop** – where a horse stops instantly – was developed by cowboys so that they could come to a rapid halt when galloping toward a precipice!

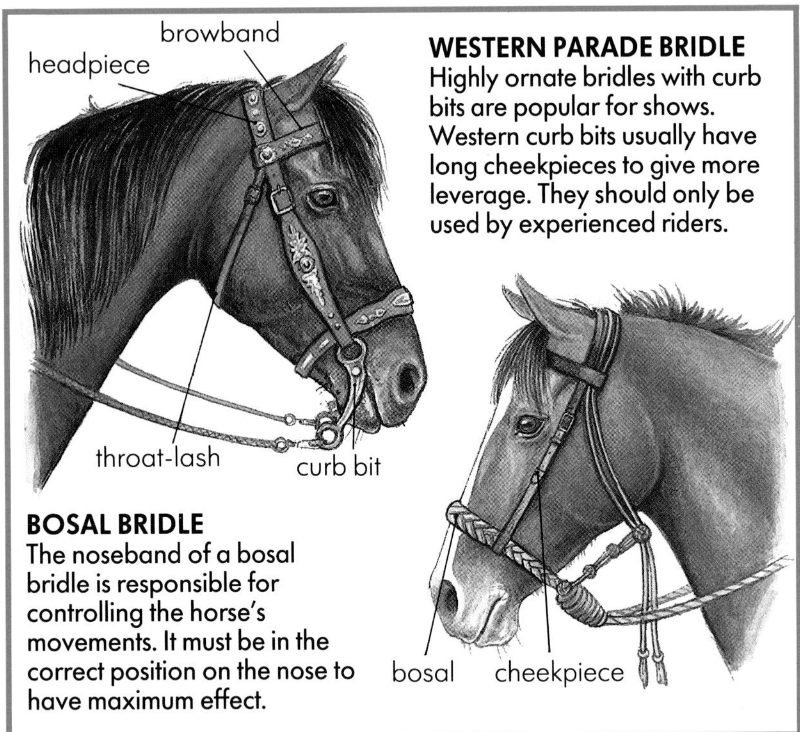

WESTERN PARADE BRIDLE
Highly ornate bridles with curb bits are popular for shows. Western curb bits usually have long cheekpieces to give more leverage. They should only be used by experienced riders.

BOSAL BRIDLE
The noseband of a bosal bridle is responsible for controlling the horse's movements. It must be in the correct position on the nose to have maximum effect.

Western saddle

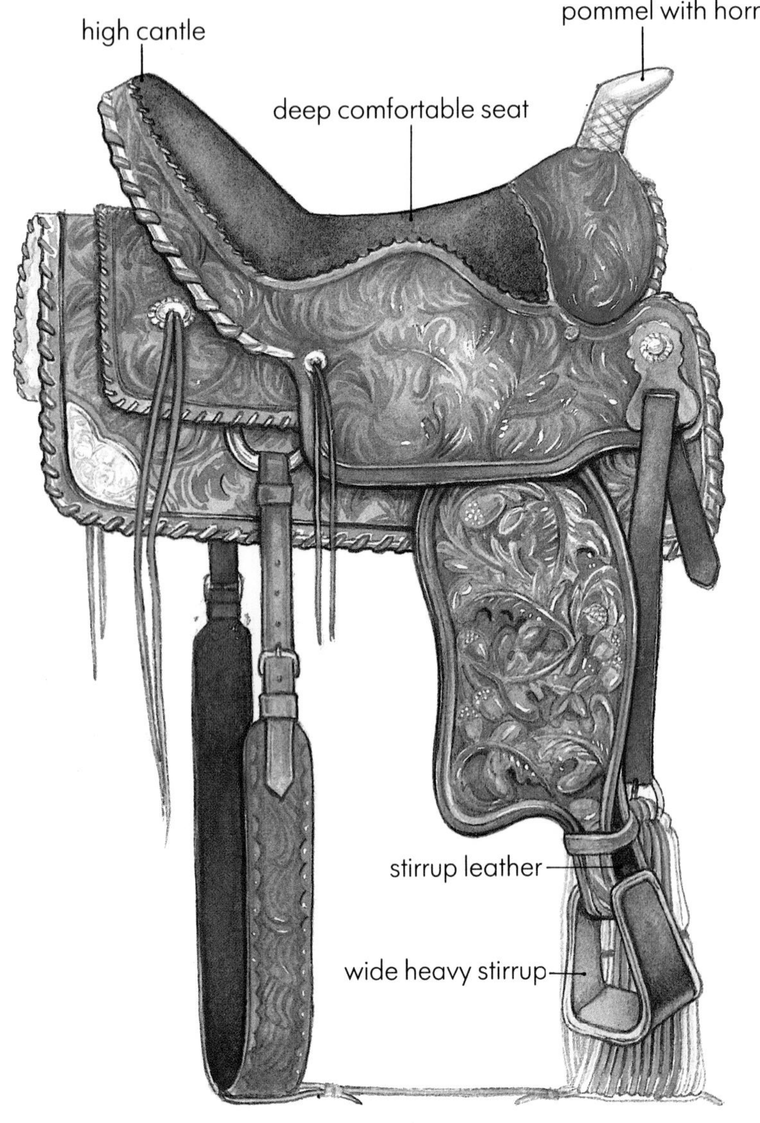

Western training involves a lot of schooling. To work well, the horse must be collected with his hindlegs well under his body. He should keep to a steady pace so he does not get tired.

Western tack

Western tack can be plain or highly decorative for parades. The saddle is hard wearing and comfortable and the bridle is designed for easy repair.

The Western saddle is heavy but it is constructed so that the weight is distributed evenly over the horse's back. To make it comfortable for the horse, blankets and pads are placed under the saddle to cushion the weight.

The saddle is extremely tough. Ranch hands often need to single out one steer from a herd. They do this by lassoing the animal with a rope attached to the saddle horn. So the saddle must be strong enough to take the strain of the extra weight.

The bosal bridle is the original bitless bridle (hackamore). The horse is controlled by pressure put on the soft part of the nose rather than on the mouth. The reins are traditionally made from hair rope and they are attached to the plaited rawhide noseband (bosal).

Fine leather parade bridles are popular in the show ring. The leather is mounted with superb silver decorations, and the bit is sometimes inlaid with silver.

Western reins can be up to 2m (7ft) long. They are either joined or split. Split reins are made up of two separate strips of leather which do not join at the end. Joined reins, on the other hand, have a length of leather added to the end. This is called a *romal* and can be used as a riding whip.

The Western seat

The position in the Western saddle is similar to that of the classical seat except that the stirrup leathers are longer.

The rider sits in the deepest part of the saddle with a straight back and square shoulders. The legs should be almost straight – allowing about 5cm (2in) between the rider and the saddle when standing in the stirrups.

A balanced, independent seat is essential in Western riding. The looser contact with the horse's mouth tends to encourage a firm seat.

Mounting

1 Stand *facing* the left-hand side of the horse. Place your left hand, holding the reins, on the horse's neck. Put your left foot into the stirrup.

2 Hold the pommel with your right hand and push yourself off the ground. Bring your left knee against the saddle and balance on your left foot.

3 Swing your right leg up and over the horse and land gently in the saddle. Place your right foot in the right stirrup.

◄ **Just as for classical riding**, there should be a straight line from the shoulder through the hip to the heel.

Sit upright in the saddle but stay relaxed – let supple knee and ankle joints absorb the movement of the horse.

Dismounting

1 Holding the reins, place your left hand on the horse's neck and put your right hand on the pommel. Take your right foot only out of the stirrup.

2 Lift your right leg up over the saddle, keeping your left foot in the stirrup. Your right leg may catch on the cantle if you free both feet.

3 When your right foot touches the ground you can then take your left foot out of the stirrup.

Tacking up

The special saddlery for Western riding requires slightly modified methods of tacking up, but the basic rules still apply – the pony must be comfortable in tack that is appropriate and fits correctly.

Bridling the pony

Depending on which type you use, you have to get used to putting on bridles with no bit and possibly no browband either (the bosal), or to handling a curb bit correctly (parade bridle).

The bosal (hackamore) slips over the nose like a headcollar, but the rawhide noseband, which is heavy and fairly stiff, must be put on with care. If it is too high, it doesn't do its job, and if it is too low, the horse can't breathe properly.

The bosal may be of the browband or split-ear variety. The split-ear bridle has no browband, but the headpiece has a split on one side through which you pull the pony's ear.

Parade bridle: Stand by the left side of the pony's head. Take off the headcollar and buckle it around his neck so that he can't walk away. If the bridle has joined reins, put them over the pony's head. With split reins, place them over the pony's neck (on either side), or knot the reins to join them together and put them over his head.

Put your right hand between the horse's ears and hold the headpiece. Take the bit in your left hand, and gently slip it into his mouth.

Ease the pony's ears under the headpiece and pull his forelock over the browband. Finally, buckle the throatlash, leaving it fairly slack: there should be about a fist's width between the strap and the throat.

If the bridle has a curb bit, this will have either a leather curb strap or a curb chain. Slip the leather curb strap over the chin as you insert the bit. If it has a curb chain, you have to leave this unhooked until the bridle is in place, then twist it until all the links lie flat before hooking it up. Both curb straps and chains must be loose enough to make contact with the curb (chin) groove *only* when the reins are pulled. Always unhook the curb chain before you remove the bridle.

Your hands

When you begin Western riding you hold the reins in two hands just as for English (Classical style) riding. This helps you to maintain the correct position in the saddle by keeping the shoulders and body straight and square. Two-handed riding is also essential when training the young Western horse.

The experienced Western rider, however, has only one hand on the reins to leave the other free for work such as roping. Also, in the Western show ring

◄ **For long treks,** the Western style is a comfortable way of riding. This trail rider is setting out from the Gold Canyon Ranch in Arizona, North America.

★ **SPECIAL REINS**

The *mecate* (hair rope) reins of the bosal are made from one length of rope. They are wrapped around the heel knot of the noseband under the horse's chin.

To alter the size of the noseband, you make a larger or smaller number of wraps. You coil the excess length of rope neatly and tie it on the left side of the saddle to the front saddle strings.

Putting on different bridles

▲ **The split-ear** has a loop through which the horse's right ear slots. This makes the bridle secure enough not to need a browband or throat-lash (but some do have a throat-lash).

▲ **Bosals with browbands** are put on over the nose, like a headcollar or halter. The noseband should already be adjusted to fit the horse, as it must be correctly positioned.

▲ **Parade bridles** are decorated with pieces of silver and are heavier than a normal bridle. Great care is needed to be sure they fit correctly.

the rider must ride with one hand and not change the reins from hand to hand. If you are right-handed you hold the reins in your left hand, and vice versa.

Hold your rein-hand just above the level of the saddle horn, and position it either over or just in front of the horn. When riding one-handed you have to take care not to let the shoulder of the rein-hand come forward, which would twist your body.

Holding the reins

When riding one-handed, joined reins including the romal (the length of leather attached to the reins, for use as a whip) come up through the bottom of your hand and out over the index finger. The romal is held in your other hand which rests on your thigh.

Split reins may be held in two ways. They can either come up through the bottom of the hand, like the joined reins, but with the excess rein left to lie down the horse's shoulder. Or, they can come down over the top of the hand and out at the bottom. In this case the index finger can be inserted between the reins or not, as the rider chooses.

In all cases your thumb lies on top of the reins to act as a brake and to prevent the reins from being pulled through your hand.

With split reins, the best positions for your free hand are either straight down by your side or resting on your thigh. Wherever the free arm is, it should be as still as possible.

How to saddle up

1 Stand on the left side of the pony. Place the pad and/or blanket on his withers. Slide them back into position so the hairs underneath lie flat.

2 With the stirrups and cinch (girth) over the seat of the saddle, put your left hand in the gullet under the fork, and hold the rear saddle skirts with your right hand. Lift the saddle gently on to the pony's back.

3 Holding the horn, give the saddle a little shake so that it settles into the right place. Lift the blanket into the gullet to let air reach the pony's back.

4 Make sure that the cinch is not twisted. Pass the latigo (the leather strap that secures the cinch) through the cinch ring and tie or buckle to secure.

1

2

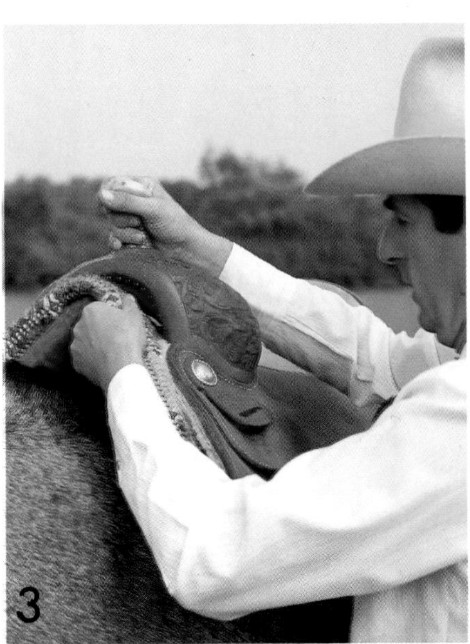
3

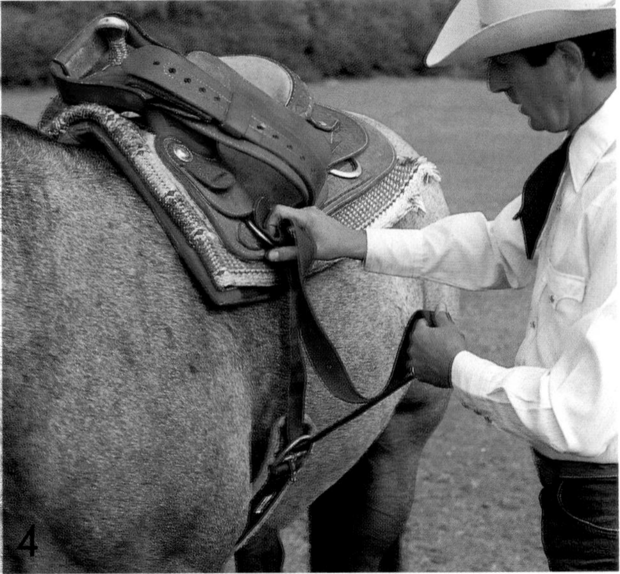
4

How to hold the reins

Joined reins with romal: The reins come up through the bottom of your hand and out over your index finger, with your thumb on top. Hold the romal in your other hand and rest it on your thigh.

Split reins: One way of holding them is with the reins coming down over the top of your hand and out at the bottom.

Joined reins with romal

Split reins – can also be held like joined reins

▲ **Before mounting,** tighten the cinch and take the stirrups down from the seat.

Western gaits

The Western gaits allow both horse and rider to stay comfortable and save energy when covering long distances or working long hours.

Slowing the pace

Western gaits differ from those of English riding in the following ways:

- They are performed more slowly.
- Western gaits are carried out with the horse's feet remaining very close to the ground. A high-stepping leg action is tiring for both horse and rider if performed for a long time.
- A Western horse rarely gallops. The gallop is used only for short spurts when working cattle.

These differences developed for practical reasons. The early American cowboy spent hours – even days – in the saddle, and the long stirrups combined with the smooth movements of the horse meant he could sit upright and still in the saddle at all paces.

The walk

The Western horse should swing along at a free-striding, lively walk and show no signs of laziness. To ask for the walk, close both legs with an even pressure on the horse's sides, and give with your rein hand, until he walks forward.

To maintain a good walk, use alternate leg aids – as the right foreleg comes back you use your right leg, and as the left foreleg comes back you use your left leg. Your rein hand yields to the head-bobbing movement of the horse when at the walk.

The jog

The jog is a slow trot that the horse can maintain easily for quite a distance. You do not rise to the jog, but stay seated as for sitting trot, with your back absorbing the movement.

To ask for the jog, close both legs on the horse's sides, a little more firmly than when asking for walk. Once the pony is jogging, the leg pressure should be reinforced only if he tries to slow down or come back to walk. The pony's head movement is very slight at the jog, so your rein hand remains still.

Even though the pony's feet stay close to the ground, they should not be dragging along. The jog is not just a shuffling trot – the pony should still work with plenty of impulsion and place his hindlegs well under his body.

▲ ► **The Western paces** are comfortable, low-stepping gaits. However, they still need plenty of engagement of the hindlegs – the horse does not just slow down and drag his feet along the ground!

The lope

The lope is the Western canter, and has the same three-time beat. Because it is slower than the canter it is more relaxed, which again makes it very comfortable for horse and rider.

As with the canter, the pony leads with one or other of his forelegs when loping. In a schooling arena or in the show ring, he must lead with his inside foreleg. This makes sure he maintains his balance when working on a circle.

The aids for the lope are the same as the classical aids. Apply your inside leg on the cinch (girth) to increase impulsion, and your outside leg behind the cinch to support the hindquarters, and give forward with the reins.

To stop the pony coming down to a jog before you want him to, apply even pressure with both legs. There is a certain amount of head movement at the lope, so your rein hand should give to this movement.

To ask your pony to slow down, or to come down from one gait to another, apply an even leg pressure and take up a contact on the reins. Use a pull-and-release action – don't pull continuously on the reins. If the pony does not respond immediately, repeat the aids.

Downward transitions should be as smooth as upward transitions, with the pony working with his hindquarters underneath him.

WESTERN CLOTHING

The Western hat provides warmth and cover from the weather.

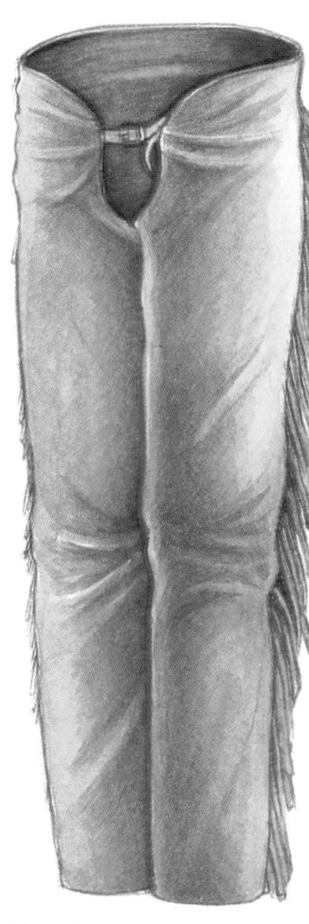

The chaps (pronounced *shaps*) are leather leggings which protect the cowboy's legs.

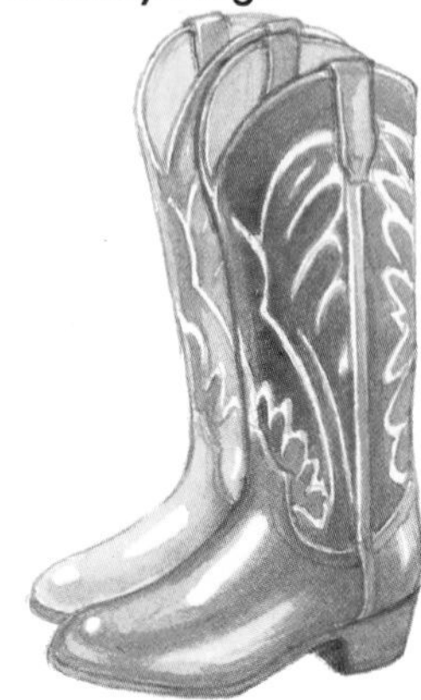

The famous high, sloped heel of the Western boot stops the foot slipping through the wide Western stirrup.

Walk to jog

1 Before you make the transition to jog, make sure the walk is energetic and the horse alert and listening to you. Keep him moving forward freely by using alternate leg aids, and have light contact on the reins.

2 Ask for the jog by squeezing both legs on the horse's sides and giving with your hands. Incline your body very slightly forward so you don't fall behind his movement when he changes pace. Note that this horse is attentive to his rider and shows no sign of resistance, while remaining calm.

3 When the horse responds to your aids, relax the pressure of your legs. Keep your back soft and supple so you can sit deep in the saddle and absorb the movement. If you stiffen your back you bounce in the saddle – making things uncomfortable for you and the horse.

Rein contact

All Western gaits are performed with the horse on a lighter rein and bit contact, and with longer reins than the classically schooled horse. This leaves the head and neck of the Western horse free so that he can use them to balance himself when working or when covering rough ground.

Although the contact is light, there *must be* a contact with the pony's mouth. Similarly, although the Western horse is not as collected as the classically schooled horse, he must still be collected and use his hindquarters to create impulsion.

Novice Western riders, particularly those who have been trained in the classical style and who are used to a close contact with the horse's mouth, may find it difficult to adjust at first. You may feel you have little or no control over the horse without shortening the reins.

This feeling disappears as you get more experienced – you soon find that the horse *does* slow down and stop when the rein and leg aids are applied. And because you rely less on the reins, Western riding tends to improve your balance – which helps your English-riding style as well.

▲ **When you are learning,** you ask for the lope from the jog, just as you do for English riding (canter from trot). With experience you can lope from the walk or halt.

Before you apply the aids for lope, the jog should be active with the horse's hindlegs stepping well under his body.

► **The lope is a slow canter** which should look smooth and flowing. Sit upright, but keep your back and waist relaxed so you absorb the movement. Keep the rein contact light, your hand giving to the movement of the horse's head.

2

3

Neck reining, reining back

Once you have mastered the Western gaits, you learn how to neck rein and rein back – two of the distinctive features of Western riding.

Neck reining

The early training of the young Western horse is started with the rider using two hands on the reins, just like the English style of riding. This is called direct reining (or plough reining).

At a later stage of his schooling the Western mount must learn to neck rein – the rider uses just one hand and turns the horse by 'drawing' the reins across his neck. The horse moves away from the pressure on his neck instead of being 'led' into the turn, as happens with direct reining.

Neck reining leaves the rider with one hand free for using a rope. Today, the working cowboy still uses a rope. In the show-ring you must also ride one-handed and neck rein.

◄ **The working cowboy** guides his horse by neck reining so he can use a rope with his free hand. This technique is firmly associated with the Western style of riding today.

Training the horse

You teach the horse to neck rein by using a combination of direct reining and neck reining, with two hands on the reins. When turning left, you pull your left hand out giving the direct rein aid. At the same time, you neck rein to the left with your right rein.

Once the horse learns to recognize the feeling of pressure on his neck as the signal to turn, you can gradually stop using the direct-reining aid.

You must give the correct leg aids at the same time as the rein signals. When turning left, apply your inside (left) leg on the cinch (girth) to 'support' the horse and give him something to bend round. Apply your outside (right) leg just behind the cinch to make sure the horse's body is bent correctly, and to stop the hindquarters swinging out.

▲ **Neck reining – literally!** This well-trained mare performs all her Western movements just as well without a bridle. The rider gives the aids using a set of reins around the horse's neck, together with leg and seat aids.

Don't try this yourself – it is only for highly skilled professionals!

◄ **The Western horse** is taught to neck rein using a combination of neck reining and direct reining.

To turn left, pull your left rein out as the direct rein aid, and at the same time press the right rein against the horse's neck. Use the leg aids as well – your left leg on the cinch (girth) for support, and your right leg just behind the cinch to control the hindquarters.

The hand movement

As a novice Western rider, you have to learn to use your neck-reining hand correctly, so you don't give the horse conflicting instructions.

When neck reining to the left, pull the rein hand (your right hand if you are right-handed) out to the left a short way, keeping your hand on the same level as the normal position. Don't move your hand up in the air, or bring it back toward your body.

If you pull your rein hand out too far, the right rein tightens, which pulls the bit on that side. This turns the horse's head to the right – completely the opposite of what is required! Make your neck-reining aids smooth and gentle; don't jerk the horse round harshly by the reins. This would only result in him throwing his head up to avoid the discomfort.

Keep your body and shoulders square when neck reining – don't let your

TRAINING TO BACK

It may be easier to teach the horse to back if, at first, the rider has an assistant on the ground tapping the horse – very gently – on the chest or forelegs with a whip.

The helper should also say 'back' clearly and firmly, while the rider gives the aids from the saddle. It is very useful if the horse learns the word 'back', because the Western horse sometimes has to obey the command to back when the rider is dismounted.

➤ **When you have learnt** how to neck rein properly at walk, practise at jog and lope – the rein and leg aids are the same at all gaits.

Practise in an enclosed arena at first, using a variety of circling and turning movements.

MISTAKES!

Don't let the shoulder of your rein hand come forward, as if 'leaning' into the turn, when neck reining. This puts a twist in your body.

Don't jerk on the reins and haul the horse round roughly. This results in evasion – the horse throws his head up because of the pain.

Avoid pulling your rein hand across too far. This has the effect of turning the horse in the opposite direction to the one you want.

shoulder 'follow' your rein hand or your body twists, which unbalances the horse.

You can practise neck reining in a school working on circles, loops, turns and serpentines. But for variety and fun, you can also practise when out riding by turning the horse around bushes and trees.

Reining back

Backing is not a natural movement for the horse, but is a very useful skill. The Western horse has to back for two reasons. First, the working horse must back to keep a rope taut when his rider has roped a cow and dismounted to tend to it. A slack rope would give the cow leeway to move or run away.

Second, the horse must back up when he does not have the space to go forward or to turn in a circle. This happens when working in rough, hilly country, and when trail riding.

Before starting to rein back, the horse should stand at halt with his hindlegs under him. He should rein back straight with his head low and flexed at the poll, and with his mouth closed.

The movement should be slow and rhythmical. The horse that 'runs' back with his head up is not reining back, but evading his rider's instructions.

Applying the aids

To rein back, first ask for a good, square halt, then squeeze with both legs to make the horse pay attention and collect himself. Apply gentle but steady pressure with the reins. Once the horse realizes that he is to move, but the hands stop him from moving forward, he should step back. Release the pressure and praise him when he does.

Increase the distance backed gradually. Apply the rein aids with a pull-and-release action, so that you are not pulling on the horse's mouth for a long period of time.

Aim to achieve a perfectly straight rein back. In Western show classes you may be penalized for backing crookedly. If the hindquarters waver to one side or the other, apply the leg aids to straighten them. If the forehand wanders, straighten it with the reins.

When the horse has backed the required distance, always ask him to walk forward at least two strides before the next movement. This makes sure that he is listening to your instructions.

▲ **Backing round a corner:** In some trail classes at shows, the horse has to back round a right-angled turn – without knocking the poles or barrier forming the angle.

For this, you use either leg aids alone, or neck reining and leg aids. In both cases, apply the same turning aids as when the horse is moving forward.

Reining back

1 Starting from a halt, get the horse's full attention by giving a little squeeze with both legs. Then apply an even pressure – gently – with your legs and the reins.

2 The horse steps back when he understands that he is required to move – but not forward. Use a pull-and-release action on the reins as you continue to back, not just a pull.

3 He should back up straight (the poles help), without resistance and with his head flexed at the poll. Try to keep a slow, steady rhythm – rather than a backward scramble!

6: Endurance Riding

▼ **If you enjoy** long rides and pony trekking, endurance riding is the sport for you.

Introduction

Endurance riding, also called long-distance riding, involves riding a set course across countryside, usually at least 34km (20 miles) long. You and your pony have to be extremely fit for this sport – it is one of the most demanding of all equestrian activities.

The basic requirements

Endurance riding is the one equestrian sport in which anyone with a sound, healthy horse or pony aged four years or older can take part. The pony's looks, dressage skills and jumping ability are not important. The major requirements are thorough preparation and a high degree of fitness, so that both you and your pony can travel happily for many hours over all kinds of terrain.

The pony must be equally content riding alone or in company. He should be relaxed and not pull too much. He should also be comfortable since you are in the saddle for many hours!

The distances

Endurance riding organizations usually have training or pleasure rides of around 17-34km (10-20 miles) for beginners or those with young horses. You get a rosette if you complete the course and your pony remains sound.

The second type of endurance ride, often called a competitive trail ride, ranges from 34-80km (20-50 miles). You have to ride at a set speed of between 10 and 14.5km (6 to 9 miles) per hour, mostly at a trot. So at 10km (6 miles) per hour you could complete a 34km (20 mile) ride in 3 hours 20 minutes.

Your pony has to undergo a veterinary inspection before the ride to make sure he is fit enough to start. He then has several veterinary inspections along the way to check that he has not become injured or exhausted. A final veterinary inspection after the ride is over checks that he finishes as healthy and sound as when he started.

Endurance rides of 80-160km (50-100

▲ **You are allowed** to dismount and walk with your pony at any time on the course, if you want to give him a breather or stretch your legs.

However, most rides have a maximum time limit, so you should beware of losing too much speed.

SPONSORED RIDES
You can find out if you and your pony might enjoy endurance riding by taking part in a sponsored ride for charity.

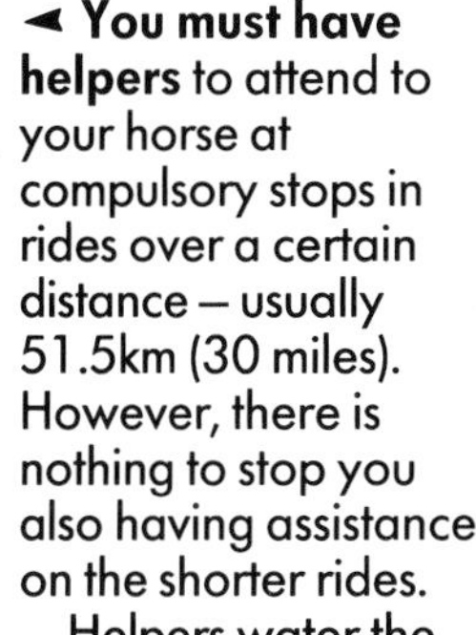

◄ **You must have helpers** to attend to your horse at compulsory stops in rides over a certain distance – usually 51.5km (30 miles). However, there is nothing to stop you also having assistance on the shorter rides.

Helpers water the horse and sponge him down, and check his pulse and respiration. They inspect his legs, feet and shoes, and adjust tack as necessary.

They also attend to you – with much-needed refreshments!

Veterinary inspection

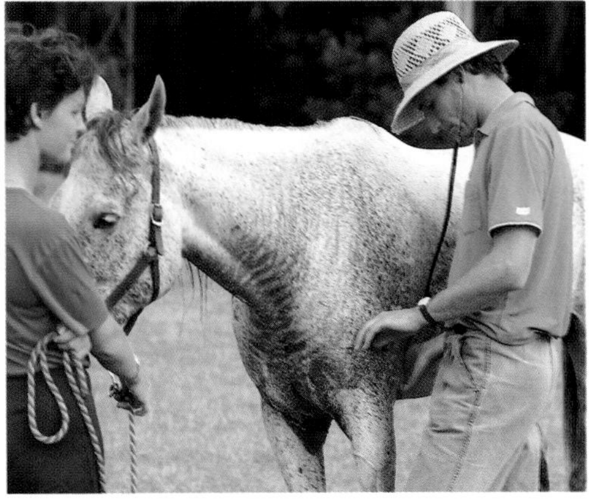

In all endurance rides, your pony has several veterinary inspections. These are at the start and finish, and at set points along the route to check that he is fit to continue.

The inspections are thorough and strict to make sure that no horse suffers.

In race rides, and some of the 80-160km (50-100 mile) rides, penalty points are given for minor changes in fitness compared to the start of the ride, such as a slight change in your pony's pulse or respiration rate. A very high rate results in elimination, as does lameness.

However, even though your pony is checked by a vet, you yourself must be able to recognize when he is too tired to continue. The welfare of the pony must always come first.

► **At international competitions** there might be a minimum weight allowed in your category; this is to make it fair for everyone. If you and the tack do not reach this, you have to carry a number of lead weights.

miles) are much tougher and require a much greater level of fitness. To take part in a long endurance ride, you usually have to qualify by completing a certain number of shorter rides first.

Race rides

Most endurance rides provide rosettes, certificates or trophies to any horse and rider who finish within the allowed time and pass the final veterinary inspection. This means that you are competing against yourself and not against other riders.

However, there is one category of endurance ride, the race ride, in which the fastest horse wins. These rides are very exciting in the last stages, with horses often galloping flat out.

Your time includes some compulsory halts, and any veterinary penalty points (for minor fitness changes, such as an alteration in the pony's pulse or respir-

ation rate) are recorded as minutes added to the riding time. There may be different prizes awarded according to the number of penalty points you incur.

Varied terrain

Rides take place over varied, natural countryside. Although there are no man-made jumps, you may have to pop over logs, streams or ditches. You have to ride up and down steep hills, and negotiate uneven, stony paths and wide streams. There may also be rivers or ponds to wade through – sometimes horses even have to swim!

Bad weather can be the biggest obstacle of all, as you may find yourself riding in extreme conditions such as heavy rain, cold or heat.

Getting fit

Riding long distances, particularly over rough, hilly country, can be extremely tiring – especially as most of the endurance ride is done in trot.

A well-planned fitness programme and enough training of both you and your pony are essential if you want to compete. Your pony's muscles must be built up slowly. This is achieved through many hours of walking and trotting, long sessions of roadwork and riding up and down hills.

You also need to practise over the same type of ground as you cover in competitions. Riding round an indoor school or on a flat bridlepath every day won't prepare you or your horse for tackling steep hills or rocky paths.

You must be fit enough, too. If you get very tired before the ride is finished, you are likely to start riding poorly. When you slouch you make it harder for your pony to carry you. Also, you need to be alert to guide your pony through any stretches of rough terrain.

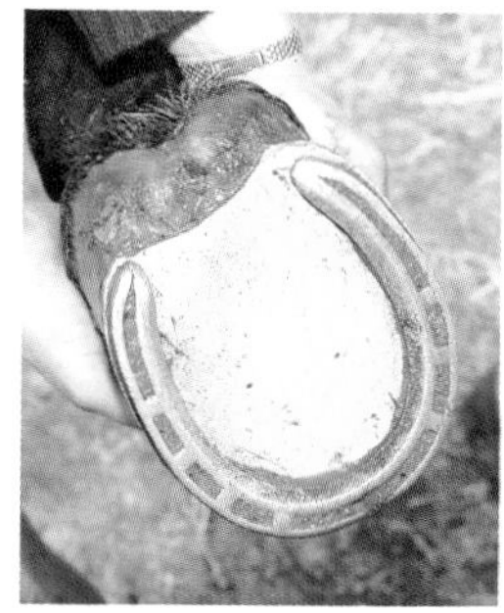

▲ **Some horses** have special pads fixed to the undersides of their feet. These prevent damage to the sole of the foot on hard or stony ground.

▲ **Use plenty of protective padding** underneath the saddle to relieve pressure on your pony's back and prevent sores. This rider is using a thick pad underneath a sheepskin numnah.

The saddle must fit the pony correctly – and also be comfortable for you.

◄ **Be prepared** for many different kinds of terrain – endurance riding is not like going for a quiet hack!

Taking part

▼ **Long-distance riding** is a sport that is open to everybody, young and old. It provides the challenge of competing against other riders while riding across beautiful countryside.

You can try pleasure rides at first to find out if you like the sport. Then you can attempt longer distances as your pony's fitness improves.

Long-distance riding is a fast growing, popular sport. You can make it challenging by competing with other riders, or you can simply enjoy a pleasant country ride. Most ponies are suitable for this sport, and they sometimes have special classes.

Endurance organizations

Rides are run by three groups in Britain: the British Endurance Riding Association (BERA), the Endurance Horse and Pony Society of Great Britain (EHPS) and the Scottish Endurance Riding Club.

They organize endurance rides, which are really races over distances of up to 160km (100 miles) in one day. Competitive trail rides are also organized, where you ride a certain distance at a set speed. The distances vary between 34–80km (20–50 miles). Pleasure rides of up to 34km (20 miles) are held too, so there's something to please everyone.

Junior riders take part in the same competitions as adults, and must qualify their ponies in the same way. The EHPS, however, has a junior section with separate points, trophies and awards.

Veterinary checks

The welfare of the horse is the most important consideration in all distance rides. For this reason, veterinary inspections are carried out before the start, after the finish, and sometimes during the ride.

Any horse failing to meet the veterinary requirements is 'spun' (eliminated). The two most common reasons for eliminating a horse are lameness, and a pulse

rate which is too high. A pulse of more than 64 beats a minute is a sign of tiredness.

In competitive trail rides, your pony may be given penalties for problems such as a bruised mouth or an overreach. In endurance rides, there are no penalties; the vet judges simply whether your pony is fit to continue.

Prizes for all

All endurance rides have awards and rosettes for everyone whose horse finishes the ride and passes the veterinary inspections. The motto of the European Endurance Rides Conference is 'To complete is to win'. This sums up what the sport is all about. Serious endurance riders like the competitive aspect of racing. Other people simply enjoy distance riding for the challenge of completing a tough course.

Starting off

You can find out if you enjoy the sport by taking part in pleasure rides, which are non-competitive events open to anyone. They are usually about 34km (20 miles) long and ridden at a speed of at least 8kmh (5mph). Most horses who are fit enough for hunting, Pony Club or Riding Club activities should certainly be able to manage this quite easily.

Once you decide you want to do more distance riding, the next step is to train your pony and progress through the various distances and speeds until you become qualified to take part in proper endurance rides. This should be done over at least two seasons.

►**You must trot your horse** in-hand during the veterinary inspection so he can be checked for lameness.

▼**Vary your training** by bringing your horse to a beach, lake or stream. Riding through water is very good for a horse's legs: it develops muscle and strengthens tendons. Making him familiar with water also ensures that he won't be frightened if you have to cross a stream during your competition ride.

Suitable ponies

You don't need a special type of pony to begin endurance riding, but some types are more suitable than others for the longer distances.

Arab horses are the most popular breed for this sport, so a pony with some Arab blood is a good choice. Arabs are renowned for their stamina and endurance. They are usually forward going and have a long stride which helps them cover the distances easily.

Thoroughbred horses are sometimes used, but refined Thoroughbred ponies are not suitable. A good combination is some Thoroughbred blood in a native pony. The Thoroughbred adds speed to the native pony's natural stamina.

Welsh ponies and Welsh pony or cob crosses make excellent endurance ponies. They are active, keen and have both stamina and hardiness. Other native breeds that do well in distance riding are Connemara and New Forest ponies. These ponies are renowned for their surefootedness.

Horses and ponies must be at least four years old before they can begin distance work and cannot compete in 160km (100 mile) rides until they are six or seven. This depends on the rules of the organizers. Most top riders believe it takes three years to train a horse to serious endurance riding level.

Conformation

Show horse conformation is not essential for this sport. Your horse can compete as long as he has some athletic ability and scope for movement. This means he should have a long sloping shoulder, with room at the elbow, a long well-muscled forearm, large flat knees and short cannon bones.

◄ **You should give your pony** a rest at some time during the competition. He may like a drink or he might just want to take a breather!

▲ **Dismounting often** helps a tired pony tackle a difficult descent. You must be mounted, however, when you go through the start and the finish.

The hindlegs should have a good length from the point of the hip to the hock, with a well-defined stifle joint and a well-developed second thigh. The hocks should be large and strong.

The pasterns should not be too upright or too sloping. There should be a straight line from the pastern, running down the hoof to the ground.

A pony who is going to succeed at distance riding must enjoy his work and competitions. He needs a keen attitude to keep him going when he is tired. He should be alert and interested in his surroundings, but have a calm temperament so that his pulse rate doesn't rise from excitement at veterinary inspections. If your pony fits this description, why not have a go?

Endurance riding: training

◄**A high level of fitness** is needed for the longer endurance rides. You can start with the shorter rides and build up to the longer distances.

It's a good idea to dismount for a while during the ride to stretch your legs and give your horse a rest.

Training your pony for distance riding takes more time than for other equestrian sports. Before he tackles the longer rides, he needs to become really fit. This means building up your pony's stamina gradually for several months.

Early training

The long-distance riding season begins in spring so much of your training has to be done in the winter months when the days are shorter. You can train the pony yourself – though it probably means early mornings for you!

If you aim to begin the competitive season with a 32km (20 mile) ride, an hour's work three or four days a week with two longer rides at the weekends is sufficient. One weekend ride should be 24–32km (15–20 miles) long and the other 16–24km (10–15 miles) long.

Because you ride at a set speed in competitions, most of this training needs to be done at the trot. Make full use of bridleways and common land as too much trotting on the road can cause strains and concussions.

To progress to a 64km (40 mile) ride, you need to build up your pony's work to about 112km (70 miles) a week. During this stage he should be ridden six days a week. Aim to complete one shorter ride of 13–16km (8–10 miles), three rides of 16–24km (10–15 miles) and one long ride of 40–48km (25–30 miles) each week.

Try to do your last long training ride a week before the competition. Work at a faster speed than you will need to in the actual competition, so that the pony manages the event easily.

Checking fitness

During your pony's training, you can keep a check on his fitness by taking his heart rate with a stethoscope. Your vet can show you how to use it.

First take your pony's heart rate while he is quiet in his stable before exercise. This is known as his 'resting' rate and it may fall slightly as he becomes fitter. A fit pony's pulse is between 36 and 42 beats per minute.

When he is exercised at speed, your pony's heart rate increases rapidly and may reach 200 beats or more per minute.

▼**Ride your horse** through as much varied terrain as possible during training. If he's used to all kinds of countryside he won't be surprised at a competition.

►**Check your pony's shoes** before you enter a competition. There is usually a farrier on hand at the larger events to replace a shoe if your pony loses one during the ride.

When you stop work and dismount, it drops down quickly to around 60 beats per minute. If you take it again 10 minutes later, it should be almost back to its normal rate.

The time it takes for the heart rate to return to normal after exercise is called the 'recovery rate'. Your pony's fitness can be gauged by how quickly this happens. The faster his pulse rate returns to normal, the fitter he is.

Fat versus condition

Keep your feeding routine simple. As your pony works harder, he needs more concentrate feed. You can judge how much more he needs by keeping an eye on his condition. As he becomes fitter, he loses any fat and his muscles become harder and more defined.

What you feed depends on many factors, from his type and breed to his temperament – generally, avoid too many oats if he hots up, and barley if he is inclined to put on weight.

Keep your pony's increase in exercise in proportion to the increase in his food. Too much food with too little exercise during the week, followed by a major outing at the weekend, could lead to circulation problems.

Many ponies tend to become overweight easily. A fat pony finds it more difficult to work hard than one who is in good condition. Watch your pony carefully to make sure he doesn't put on any excess weight.

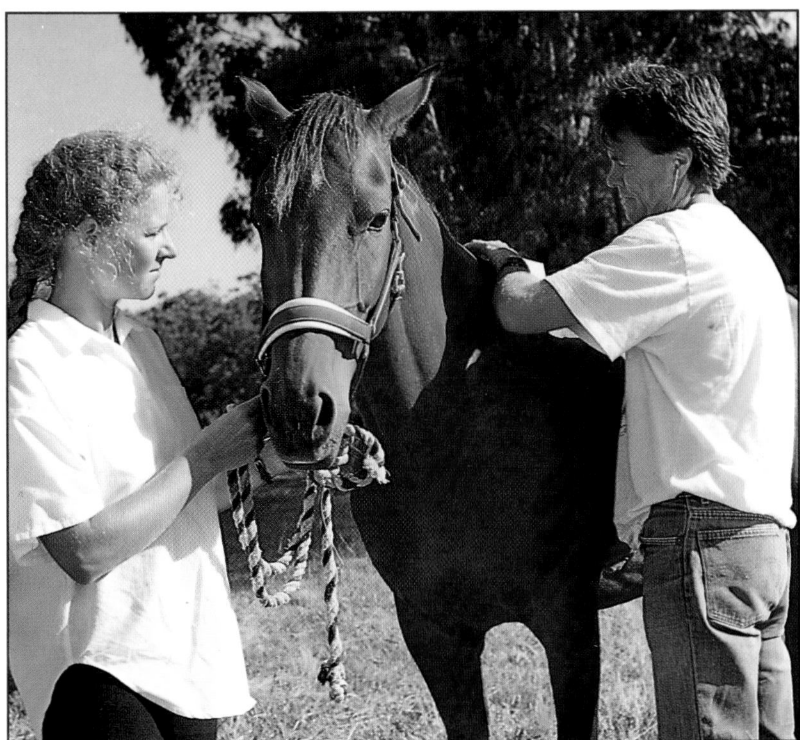

▼**At the first vetting,** your pony's pulse is checked and recorded. He is also trotted out to see if he's sound.

Study the route

Before a competition you will receive a copy of the route. Study this carefully. An Ordnance Survey map of the area may also be of help to you.

Routes are designed to include as much good going and interesting countryside as possible. The terrain may be chalk downland, heather upland, forest tracks or bridleways. If you include as many different sorts of countryside as you can on your training rides, your pony won't be surprised by new terrain during a competition.

Jumping is not included – except perhaps for an occasional log across the path – but there are almost always stream or river crossings, so your pony should be used to water.

It is well worth accustoming the pony to as many unusual sights and sounds as possible during training. You never know what you might meet on a long-distance ride – you could see anything from horse-drawn vehicles to hang gliders while you're out!

Veterinary check

Arrive at the competition in good time – you can be penalized for presenting your pony late to the vet. Collect your number and prepare your pony. For the inspection he should wear a headcollar or a bridle but not his saddle. Put his rug on if it is chilly. Don't oil his hooves, as the vet picks up his feet. Imagine picking up 400 oiled hooves!

At this first vetting, your pony's pulse is taken and recorded, he is checked over for lumps and bumps and trotted up to see if he is sound. You should declare any recent minor injuries to the vet. His shoes are also checked, so be sure they are fairly new and have no loose nails.

After your pony has been checked by the vet, tack him up – his tack is inspected at British Horse Society Long Distance Group rides.

This vetting procedure is repeated 30 minutes after the finish of all rides and at various stages during the longer rides. To pass the vetting, your pony's pulse rate must not be more than 64 beats per minute. Lameness means elimination and serious back, girth or mouth lesions may also mean your pony is judged not 'fit to continue' by the vet.

▲**Cantering uphill** is an important part of any fitness programme. It strengthens a horse's lungs and improves muscle tone.

◄**The route** of most long-distance rides takes you through water. Your horse should be used to crossing streams and rivers before taking part in a competition.

In some countries it is not compulsory to wear a hard hat while competing. Check the rules carefully to see what you can wear.

Endurance riding : competing

►**Part of the equipment** you must take with you is a map with the course clearly marked. A quick look at the map tells you how many miles you have covered and how many you still have in front of you – this gives you some indication of how fast you should ride.

▼**It's a good idea** to put brushing boots on your horse to prevent him hurting himself and risking elimination by the vet. You may have to remove them for the vet checks.

Once your horse is totally fit you can enter him in competitive trail rides and longer endurance events. To give yourself the best chance of success you need to study the course carefully before the ride and have an efficient back-up crew to save you time at the vet checks.

The briefing

The evening before a long-distance ride there is a preliminary vetting to check that the horses are perfectly sound. There is also a briefing given by the organizers – this must be attended by the competitors and the back-up crews. The route is discussed and you can ask questions about the course or the rules.

Once the briefing is over you can settle your pony for the night – most horses stay overnight for the longer classes as there is often a very early start to the competition.

Your back-up team

Long-distance riding is a team effort. To help you round the gruelling course you need a back-up crew of two or three people who know you and your pony well. It's often the ideal opportunity for members of your family to become involved in long-distance riding.

The back-up crew is in charge of taking your pony over at the compulsory halts and the finish, to give you a well-earned chance for a breather.

It is also their job to take your pony at the vet checks. An efficient crew can gain precious minutes as they decide whether your pony has recovered enough to be vetted without risk of elimination.

The crew is responsible for looking after you, too. You need a refreshing drink and perhaps something to eat to give you enough energy to carry on.

At the vet check

One crew member takes the horse and immediately offers him a drink. In hot weather electrolytes are sometimes given to replace essential minerals lost by sweating.

As soon as he has quenched his thirst, his pulse is taken with a stethoscope. ➤

◄ **Your back-up crew** plays a vital role in keeping you and your horse cool – as well as offering you both a drink, they sponge down your horse with cold water.

▼ **Pace yourself,** and show your horse consideration, during long-distance rides.

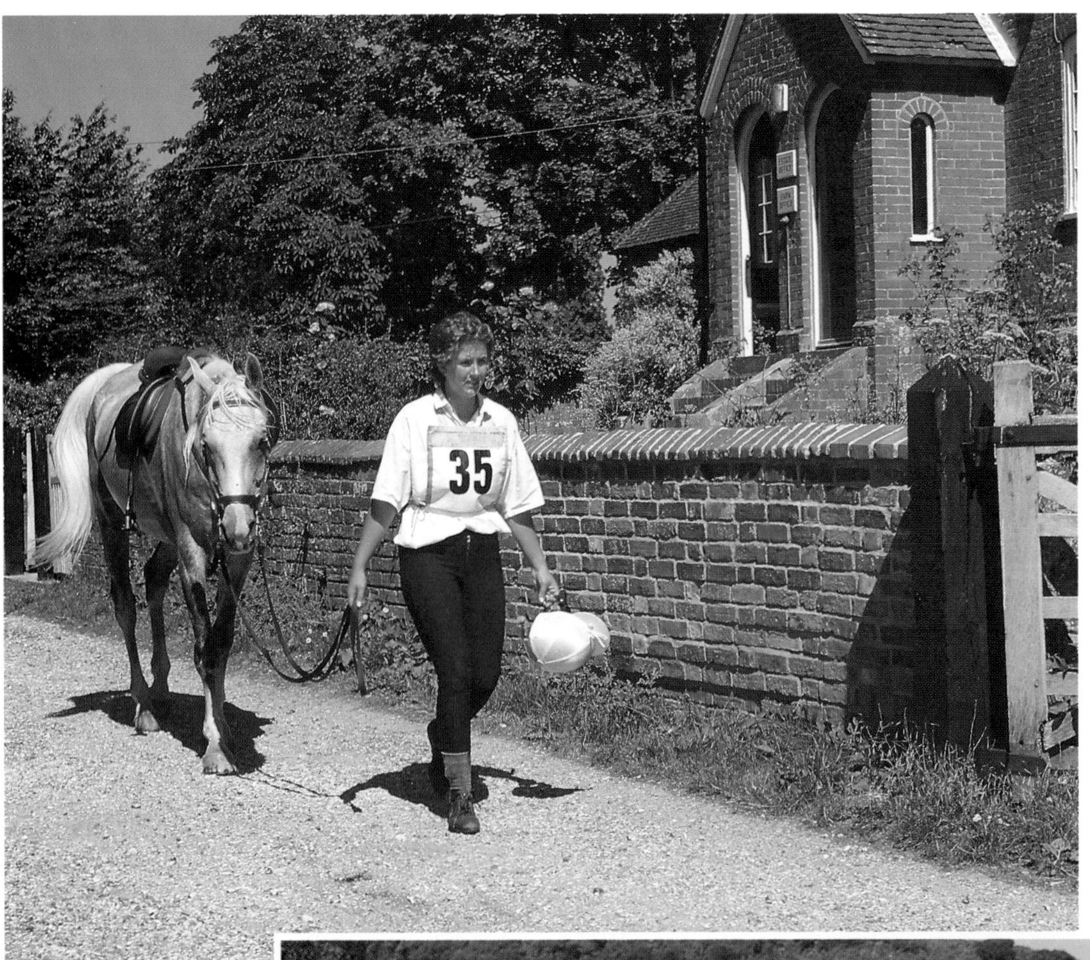

◄**Before you reach a vet check** dismount and walk your horse to allow him to cool down. His pulse rate must be less than 64 beats per minute to pass the check.

►**During the vet check** your horse is examined for cuts and bruises. He is also trotted up to test soundness. His pulse rate is taken to see if he is fit enough to cope with the rest of the ride. If he has not recovered sufficiently, he is held for 10 minutes before being tested again and then he is either passed as fit or eliminated.

If it is too high – it must be under 64 beats per minute to pass the check – a crew member sponges down the big veins on his neck and inside his legs to help him cool down.

When your horse is ready to be presented, the vet takes his pulse and checks him over for cuts and bruises. One of the crew members has to trot him past the vet so he can check for soundness – ponies often bruise a sole during the course, especially if the ground is hard. They sometimes have small cuts and grazes from stones thrown up by their hooves. Many horses are 'spun' (eliminated) by the vet because they're not quite sound and could get worse.

If the vet thinks that your pony hasn't recovered enough to continue the ride, he is put in a holding pen for 10 minutes and then checked again. This gives the other competitors the chance to be on their way ahead of you if they pass the vet first time with no problems.

Coping with the ride

If you do an 80km (50 mile) ride you could be out for anything up to nine hours. The 160km (100 mile) rides have time limits of up to 24 hours.

You must help your horse when he gets tired and keep yourself going. One of the ways you can keep your weight off his back is to adopt the half seat.

To go into this position, lean slightly forward and keep your weight in your heels, flex your knees and ankles and raise your seat out of the saddle. Hover just above the saddle – don't balance yourself by pulling on the reins. Try to maintain the half seat for a few miles – time enough to give your horse a rest.

To stop your muscles seizing up, do some relaxing exercises such as swinging your legs, circling your ankles, and rolling your shoulders and neck. Attempt these exercises only when the horse is walking, and never on a road.

It's a good idea to dismount and walk beside your horse from time to time – this gives you a chance to stretch your legs and allows the horse to relax.

By pacing yourself, showing your horse consideration and finding an efficient back-up crew you can enjoy your long-distance rides – and be successful.

▼ **One way to relieve** the pressure on your horse's back is to adopt the half seat. You balance over the saddle and keep your weight in your heels. It's also a good idea to change your position from time to time to prevent your muscles becoming cramped.

Index

Note: bold page entries signify that the entry includes illustrations.

A

aids 97–8, 101–2, **187**
  dressage 97–8, 101–2
  teaching a young horse 10, 12–15
  to lengthen stride 65
all-weather arenas **21**, 22

B

bending **38**, 39, 124
bits 10
  on the bit 16–19, **18, 19**
breaking in a young horse 8–23
bridles, Western riding 177, **177**
British Dressage Preliminary Test 120–3
British Endurance Riding Association 194
British Horse Trials Association 164
British Show Jumping Association 164

C

canter 14, **15**, 22, **45**, 93, **95**
  change of leg 114, **114–15**
  and circling 27
  counter-canter 112–13, 113
  dressage 94, **95, 103**
  dressage exercises 112–15, **113–15**
  extended canter **65**, 66
  flying change **112**
  leads 53
circles 28–9, 99, **99**
clothes 132, **182**
cooling down 47, **47**, 59
course building 32, **34**, 52, 147, 167
cross country **130**, 132, 138–45
  fences 139–61
  training 147–8
  walking the course 138, **151**

D

diagonals 21–2, **23**
ditches **147, 156**
Dixon, Karen, and Get Smart **134**
dressage 93–127
  aids 97–8, 101–2
  between leg and hand 98
  canter exercises 112–115
  change of rein 97
  circling 99, **99**
  communicating 97
  impulsion and collection 102
  lateral work 104–11
  leg-yielding 107, **107**
  paces 101–2, **102–3**
  school movements 124, 126
  score sheet 127
  shoulder-in 109, **109**
  square halt 93
  tack **101**
  turn on the forehand 104–5, **104–5**
  warming up 126–7, **126–7**
  yielding to the leg 106–7, **106**
dressage arena 93
  markers 93, 117
dressage competitions 120–7
dressage test 116–27
  dressage rules 117
  test sheet 116
dressage whip 98

E

Endurance Horse and Pony Society of Great Britain 194
endurance riding 190–205
  competing 202–5
  fitness 193, 199
  ponies 196–7
  race rides 192
  training 199–201, **199**
  veterinary checks **192**, 194–5, **196**, 200–1, **200**, 203, **204**
  water **196, 201**
eventing 68–71, 130–7
see also cross country; dressage; show jumping
  the box **137**
  clothes 132
  fitness 68–9
  fitness programme 135
  one-day events 130
  roads and tracks 131–2, 135
  speed and endurance 135–7
  steeplechase 131, 135, **135**
  three-day events 130–1, 168–9
  two-day events 132
  veterinary inspection 137, 163
  walking the course 135, 138

F

feeding 41, 43, 45, 70
fences 138–45
  bounces 143, 148–9, **149, 157**
  bullfinch **142**
  coffin **156**
  combinations 140, 147–9
  corner fence 144, **145, 149**
  cross country 139–61
  distance between 32, 52, 147
  ditches **147, 156**
  drop **153**
  flags 143, 155
  height 26
  option 155, **155**
  practice fences 58
  steps **160**
  stone walls **143**
  uphill jump **157**
  water 140, **145, 152**
fitness 36–9, 68–70
flags 143, 155
flying change **112**

G

games 74–89, **74–89**
  ball and cone race 77
  ball and racket race **88–9**
  balloon bursting **79**
  fishing race **76**
  five flag race **80**
  groom's race **74**
  mug race **85**
  nine ring race 81
  organizing 74–5
  potato race **80–1**
  rope race **85**
  stepping stone dash **78**, 79
  tyre race **88–9**
gates 22, **23**
gymkhanas 36–9, 75

H

hacking out **49**
halt 10, **98**
hunting, fitness 68, **71**

I

ill health 36
impulsion 17

J

jog, Western riding 180, **182**
jumping 35, 52–9
  at an angle 32–3
  balance and control 34
  combinations 26, 28, **52**, 140, 147–9
  fitness 39
  loose **29**
  refusals 60–3
  seeing the stride 29–30, 52
  training 24–7
  walking the course **56**, 58
  and warming up **46**, 49–51
  without reins 31

L

Larrigan, Tanya, and Diplomat **108**
lateral work, dressage 104–11
leading 83–4
long distance riding,
see endurance riding
loosening up 49
lope, Western riding 180, **182**
lunge work 9, **9**, 21, **22**, 83, **126**

M

mounted games 74–89, **74–89**
choice of pony 83
games **76–81, 88–9**
neck reining 86
training 83–5

N

neck reining 86–9, 185–7, **185–7**

P

paces 66, 101–2, **102–3**
penalty system 164
piaffe **67**
plaiting the mane 56, **59**
Pony Club 40, 75, 132, **141**

Q

Quarter horse 173

R

refusing jumps 60–3
reining back **49**, 187, **187**
reins 177–8, **179**
change of rein 97
side-reins 21
renvers 22, 110–11, **111**
rhythm 17
riding in 44–5
riding out **13**
rugging up 40

S

saddles, Western 174, **174, 178**
schooling 13–18, 16, 20–3, 42
Scottish Endurance Riding Club 194
shoes (horse) 39, **193**
shoulder-in 22, **66**, 109–10
show jumping 37, 51–9
course 167, **167**
eventing 162–9
planning 56–9
training **165**
walking the course 167, **168**
warming up 168
show ponies 40–1, **41**
spoken commands 83
sponsored riding 191
spurs 98
stable management **38**
stamina 70, **70**
steeplechase 131, 135, **135**
stopping quickly 38, **173**
straightness 17
strides 52, **64**, 65–6, **65**
suppling exercises 84–5

T

tack **101, 140**, 173, **174**
Todd, Mark, on Charisma **166**
training **38–9**
interval training 70, **70–1**
routine 69
Western riding 185–7, **185–7**
young horses 8–15
transport 56
travers 22, 110, **110–11**
trot 8, 14, 93, **95**
dressage **95, 101, 103**
extended trot **64**, 66
trotting poles 24, 50, **50**
turning 10, 39

V

veterinary checks
endurance riding **192**, 194–5, **196**,
200–1, **200**, 203, **204**
eventing 137, 163

W

walk 67
dressage 94, **94**, 101, **102**
teaching the aids 10
Western riding 180
walking the course
eventing 135, 138
jumping **56**, 58, 167
walking off 43
warming up 19, 44–5, **46**, 49–51, 168
water **131**
fences 140, **145, 152**
Western riding 172–87
aids **187**
bridles 174, 177, **177**
clothing **182**
dismounting **175**
gaits 180–3
mounting **175**
neck reining 173, 185–7, **185–7**
reining back 187, **187**
reins 174, 177–8, **179**
saddle 174, **174, 178**
seat 174
sliding stop **173**
tack 173, **174**
tacking up 177–9
training 185–7, **185–7**

Y

young horses 8–23, **12**
aids 10, **10**, 12–15
cantering 14, **15**
jump training 24–7
trotting **8**, 14

Picture Acknowledgements

Photographs:
All photography by Shona Wood except the following:

Title page Allsport/Mike Hewitt; contents page Elisabeth Weiland; pages 6-7 Bob Langrish; 20 Bruce Coleman/Eric Crichton; 23(t) Martin Dalby, (b) Kit Houghton; 29 Bob Langrish; 47 Kit Houghton; 48-50 Eaglemoss/Kit Houghton; 57 Allsport/Phil Cole; 60 Elisabeth Weiland; 61 Bob Langrish; 64 Getty Images/Tony Stone/Tom Raymond; 65-66 Eaglemoss/Kit Houghton; 67 Kit Houghton; 68-69 Bob Langrish; 71(b) Eaglemoss/Bob Langrish; 72-75 Bob Langrish; 78 Bob Langrish; 79(l) Bob Langrish; 83(b) Eaglemoss/John Suett; 90-91 Allsport/Julian Herbert; 101-107 Eaglemoss/Kit Houghton; 109-115 Eaglemoss/Kit Houghton; 118(tr,b), 119, 120-121 Bob Langrish; 125 Elisabeth Weiland; 126(b) Kit Houghton; 127(tl,b) Bob Langrish; 128-129 Kit Houghton; 133(t) Bob Langrish; 134 Kit Houghton; 141(t), 142, 143 Bob Langrish; 144 Kit Houghton; 147-149, 150, 151 Bob Langrish; 152(b) Elisabeth Weiland; 153(t) Elisabeth Weiland; 154 Bob Langrish; 159 Kit Houghton; 160(t) Kit Houghton; (c) Bob Langrish; 161(b) Bob Langrish; 162-163 Kit Houghton; 166 Sandra Langrish; 170-171 Allsport; 172-174, 176-179, 184, 187(t), 188-189, 190, 191(b), 192-193 Bob Langrish; 194-195 Kit Houghton; 197(t) Kit Houghton, (b) Bob Langrish; 198 Elisabeth Weiland; 201(t) Bob Langrish, (b) Elisabeth Weiland.

Illustrations:
54-55 Denys Ovenden; 97 Coral Mula; 122-123 Eugene Fleury; 145, 155-157, 167 Denys Ovenden; 175, 182, 186 Maggie Raynor.